CHRISTIAN HER

AMY CARMICHAEL

Rescuer of
Precious Gems

D0356302

CHRISTIAN HEROES: THEN & NOW

AMY CARMICHAEL

Rescuer of Precious Gems

JANET & GEOFF BENGE

YWAM
PUBLISHING

P.O. BOX 55787   SEATTLE, WA 98155

YWAM Publishing is the publishing ministry of Youth With A Mission. Youth With A Mission (YWAM) is an international missionary organization of Christians from many denominations dedicated to presenting Jesus Christ to this generation. To this end, YWAM has focused its efforts in three main areas: (1) training and equipping believers for their part in fulfilling the Great Commission (Matthew 28:19), (2) personal evangelism, and (3) mercy ministry (medical and relief work).

For a free catalog of books and materials, call (425) 771-1153 or (800) 922-2143. Visit us online at www.ywampublishing.com.

Amy Carmichael: Rescuer of Precious Gems
Copyright © 1998 by YWAM Publishing

13 12 11 10 09   7 8 9 10

Published by YWAM Publishing
P.O. Box 55787
Seattle, WA 98155

ISBN-13: 978-1-57658-018-9
ISBN-10: 1-57658-018-0

Printed in the United States of America.

CHRISTIAN HEROES: THEN & NOW

Unit study curriculum guides
are available for select biographies.

Available at your local Christian
bookstore or from YWAM Publishing
1-800-922-2143 / www.ywampublishing.com

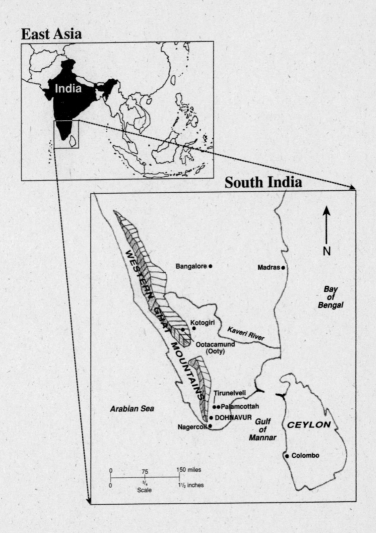

East Asia

India

South India

WESTERN GHAT MOUNTAINS

Bangalore ●

Madras ●

N

Bay
of
Bengal

Kotogiri ●

Kaveri River

Ootacamund
(Ooty)

Tirunelveli
●●Palamcottah
● DOHNAVUR

Arabian Sea

Nagercoil ●

Gulf
of
Mannar

CEYLON

Colombo ●

0   75   150 miles
0   ¾   1½ inches
          Scale

Contents

Chapter 1

Swinging in the Rain

Waves smashed across the bow of the SS *Yokohama Maru,* sending sheets of water racing back across the deck. None of the passengers aboard noticed. They were too sick to care. Most were gathered in the ship's saloon, too scared to stay below deck as the ship shuddered and rolled violently from side to side. The smell of vomit was everywhere.

Amy Carmichael, a young Irish woman, sat in the corner sicker than she'd ever been before in her life. It felt to her as though she had been aboard ship forever, but it had been only four days. The voyage from Shanghai en route to Japan had been so calm. Halfway across the Yellow Sea, though, the ship had run into a typhoon, and as a result, she was

11

now being mercilessly battered by storm-ravaged seas. All Amy wanted to do was get her feet back on solid ground, and soon.

Just when she thought she could not stand to be thrown around by the sea any longer, the captain, wrapped in an oilskin parka, stumbled into the saloon. He spoke first in Japanese, reeling short, sharp sentences off his tongue. Then he turned to Amy and in broken English announced the good news. The *Yokohama Maru* was directly offshore from Shimonoseki, their destination port. Amy breathed a sigh of relief. Then the captain told her the bad news. Because of the wind and huge waves, there was no way the ship could dock at Shimonoseki. They would simply have to stay offshore and ride out the typhoon.

As the captain left the saloon, Amy vomited into the bucket beside her. She wondered how long they'd have to wait for the storm to die down. She felt so wretchedly ill. Still, she was tired of sitting and feeling sick, so she decided a walk might help settle her churning stomach. She knew it wouldn't, though. It hadn't any of the other times she'd tried it. Still, she had to get away from the gagging air of the saloon. She wrapped her woolen shawl around her shoulders and clambered to her feet. Stumbling out onto the deck, she took a deep breath. She gripped the ship's railing tightly as seawater washed around her ankles and spray lashed against her cheeks. She looked longingly in the direction of Shimonoseki and hoped it wouldn't be long before the wind and sea calmed enough for the ship to berth.

As she gazed towards Shimonoseki, Amy saw a most unusual sight, at least for the middle of a typhoon. A steam tugboat emerged through the blinding rain and billowing seas. It came within twenty feet of the starboard side of the SS *Yokohama Maru*, bobbing up and down in time to the waves. One of the sailors yelled to the captain, and soon a crowd of passengers and crew had spilled out on deck for a closer look.

The captain of the *Yokohama Maru* and the captain of the tugboat yelled and gestured at each other. Amy couldn't understand a word of what they said, but she hoped it had something to do with towing the SS *Yokohama Maru* into dock. But apparently, towing wasn't what they had been talking about. Instead, the captain announced that the passengers were going to be transferred to the tugboat and taken into Shimonoseki. The starboard arm of the ship's derrick was lowered, and a rope net was attached to the winch line on the derrick arm. As the first passenger was placed in the rope net and hoisted into the air, Amy looked on in horror. She wanted to get her feet on solid ground in Shimonoseki as soon as possible, but this was definitely not what she had in mind. The derrick arm swung over the side of the *Yokohama Maru* toward the tugboat. The man in the rope net looked terrified as he dangled over the frothing ocean before being dumped onto the deck of the pitching, rolling tugboat. A crewman on the tug helped the passenger out of the rope net, which was then hoisted back aboard the *Yokohama Maru* for the next passenger.

One by one, the passengers were lowered aboard the tugboat until finally it was Amy's turn. Reluctantly, she stepped into the net. Before she had a chance to change her mind, the crewman operating the winch pulled a lever, and the rope net gathered around Amy. Suddenly, she was dangling above the deck. With a jerk, the end of the derrick arm moved over the side of the ship. Amy swung like a pendulum in the rain. She looked down at the angry waves snarling up at her. Frothy spray soaked through her clothes. Then she was over the aft deck of the tug, and as she swung from side to side, the winch slowly lowered her. One of the tug's crewmen grabbed the net and steadied it as Amy was dumped bottom first onto the deck. The crewman helped her out of the net, and she huddled with the other passengers.

Finally, when all the passengers had been lowered aboard the tug, their luggage was also loaded into the net and transferred to the tugboat. After some more yelling between the captain of the tugboat and the captain of the *Yokohama Maru*, and a loud hoot of the tug's steam horn, the two boats parted.

If the trip on the *Yokohama Maru* had been treacherous, the ride on the tugboat was downright dangerous. Amy prayed frantically throughout the journey. The small tug didn't cut through the stormy seas like the larger ship had. Instead, it rode up and over the mountainous waves. At the crest of each wave, the tug tipped forward or rolled sideways so much that Amy thought it would capsize for sure. Finally, the outline of the Japanese coast came into view, and a cheer went up from the passengers.

Amy's feet were soon back on solid ground. As the rain dripped from her felt hat and formed rivulets that ran down her cotton dress, she breathed a deep breath and slowly exhaled. For the first time in several days, she didn't feel like vomiting. She had made it to Japan. She had traveled halfway around the world, and now she was finally here. What an adventure it had been! There had been so many risks along the way. But then, risks and adventure were nothing new to Amy Carmichael. She'd always been willing to take risks to get what she wanted.

Chapter 2

Shadows in the Attic

Amy—Amy Carmichael. Are you listening?" Amy looked up at the teacher and scrambled to get her mind back on trigonometry. But the truth was, she hadn't been listening for quite a while. She had more important things than math on her mind. It was September 12, 1882, a once-in-a-lifetime day, and Amy was not about to miss the event! How cruel it had been of the astronomy teacher to tell his students all about the "great September comet," when he knew none of the girls at Marlborough House boarding school would be allowed to stay up to watch it. Amy had tried everything she could think of to get around the rule that dormitory girls were not allowed to stay up past 9 P.M. But nothing had made any difference. She had even gone to

Miss Kay, the school principal, and begged her to let the girls stay up. But comet or no comet, Miss Kay had no intention of bending the rules one bit.

Amy hadn't wanted to ask Miss Kay, but as usual, she had been the one voted to do it. Being only fourteen years old meant there were lots of older girls in the school, but Amy was a natural leader. She had courage the other girls envied. Even when she'd knocked firmly on Miss Kay's door, she hadn't been one bit afraid. And when Miss Kay dismissed what Amy thought was a well-balanced argument for being allowed to stay up to view the comet, Amy had left the office with her head held high. The other girls were depending on her, and she would find another way for them to watch the comet.

That was the problem occupying her mind during trigonometry class. As she thought about it, a plan began to form in her mind. *What was to stop them from sneaking up and watching the comet from the attic skylight?* That way they wouldn't even have to go outside, and if they were very quiet, the dormitory mistress wouldn't hear them. It was a plan Amy was sure would work. Now all she had to do was figure out a way to keep the other girls awake until midnight. Amy knew she could stay awake herself; the excitement of seeing a comet wouldn't let her sleep. But if some of the other girls fell asleep, it would be hard to wake them, and it could be noisy, too.

By the time the girls were all dressed in their long, white flannel nightgowns ready for bed, Amy knew just how they'd do it. She cleared her throat, twisted her long, dark brown hair behind her head, and told the girls about her disappointing visit to Miss Kay. Several of the girls hung their heads. Amy paused a moment for dramatic effect, and then she produced a reel of sewing thread she'd sneaked from embroidery class. "This is our answer," she said jubilantly, holding the thread in the air. The girls looked puzzled.

Again Amy paused for effect before going on. "Everyone will get a long piece of thread. After the lamps are blown out, you will tie one end of it to your big toe."

A ripple of giggles flowed from the girls.

Amy continued. "After you have tied the thread to your big toe, creep over to me and give me the other end and go back to bed. I will hold the other end of all of the pieces of thread and tug on them every so often to keep you all awake. When I hear the bells chime out twelve o'clock, I'll give a double tug on the thread. That will be the signal. We'll all get out of bed and creep up to the attic and watch the comet through the skylight. Just be sure to skip the third step on the way up the stairs. It creaks."

The girls all giggled and nodded and set about tying the thread to their big toes. Every so often, after the lamps were blown out, Amy jerked the threads to keep everyone awake. Finally, the clock struck twelve, and Amy gave the threads a double tug. The girls all sat up straight in bed and untied the thread from their big toes. Quietly, they formed a line by the door. They did this without even thinking, because everywhere they went at boarding school, from chapel to dinner, they walked in a line. They filed out the door, past the dormitory mistress's room, and up the stairs. Each girl stepped carefully over the third step. They all glided up to the attic like a silent row of ghosts. With great care, Amy turned the brass knob on the huge oak door at the top of the stairs. The knob didn't squeak. Amy slowly pushed the door open and motioned the girls to go in. Once the door was shut behind them, the girls gathered in silence under the skylight.

As her eyes adjusted to the dim moonlight that spilled into the attic through the skylight, Amy had an odd feeling. She looked around. The attic was filled with shapes. There were the shapes of old furniture and piles of books, but there were some other shapes, too, clustered in the corner. Amy peered into the darkness to make them out, and as she did, the shapes became the outlines of people. Then dread of dreads, they became the shape of Miss Kay and three other teachers.

At that moment, Miss Kay lit a candle. Several of the girls screamed. Amy's heart sank. Miss Kay would know that Amy had planned this adventure. After all, Amy planned most of the mischief that occurred at Marlborough House.

Fortunately, the comet was due to pass overhead at any moment, so Miss Kay just waved her hand at the girls, and sternly said, "Silence." And so, Amy and all the girls in her dormitory got to see the comet, but not in the company they would have liked.

Once the comet was past, Miss Kay looked directly at Amy. "I will see you in my office straight after breakfast."

"Yes, ma'am," said Amy, with a curtsy.

The girls trudged back to their room, not bothering to skip the creaking third step this time.

For the rest of the night, Amy hardly slept. She didn't mind being punished; she'd been punished plenty of times before. *But what if I'm expelled and sent back to Ireland this time? What will my parents say?* She hated the thought of going home in disgrace. Her parents would be so disappointed in her, and she had six younger brothers and sisters to set an example for. If only she weren't Irish. That was the trouble. With her flashing brown eyes and lively imagination, she just didn't seem to fit into an English girls' school. It was all too confining. Everything was done to bells and timetables. She hardly ever got to go outdoors. If it weren't for the box of chrysanthemums her mother, Catherine Carmichael, had sent her and the white lily one of the older girls had left behind, Amy would hardly get to see nature at all. It was no wonder she had to see the comet. At home in Ireland, she could have watched it from the second-story nursery window, with the Irish Sea crashing against the rocks at Millisle in the background.

How she missed the sea and the tide pools with their fresh treasures every day. And she missed her pets. At Marlborough House there was only a grumpy tomcat who spat if Amy even looked at him. Back home in Ireland there was Gildo the collie dog, who spent her days lying by the front door waiting for someone to come out and play. And Daisy, the yellow and white cat, who liked to stretch herself across the kitchen window ledge. Then there were the two ponies, Fanny and Charlie. How she loved to ride them. Three years at boarding school in England was a long time to be away from them all. Amy wished she could be back home, but she couldn't go back in disgrace. So despite feeling homesick, she hoped and prayed that Miss Kay wouldn't expel her in the morning.

As the light of dawn began to filter through the drapes, Amy still couldn't sleep. She thought back to the dollhouse she had been given for Christmas when she was eight years old. It was beautifully decorated and filled with dainty doll-sized furniture, but it was boring. On Boxing Day, the day after Christmas, she'd dumped the furniture out of the dollhouse and replaced it with moss for a carpet and twigs for indoor trees. That had made it a much more interesting place. She had gone out to the apple tree in the yard and collected ants and bugs and beetles and installed them in their new home. She had spent hours watching them climb all over it until her nanny found out and made her remove the moss and bugs. School was like the dollhouse. It was often boring, and sometimes Amy wished she could put moss down for carpet and move in some new friends and make it an interesting place.

Amy was bleary-eyed from lack of sleep as she picked at her breakfast. When everyone else had been dismissed from the dining room, she reported to Miss Kay. Unlike Amy, Miss Kay seemed to have had a good night's sleep. She was in a very good mood when Amy knocked on her door. Amy stood in front of Miss Kay's desk. Miss Kay told Amy how disappointed she was in her behavior and pointed out that Amy should use her leadership talents to lead the other girls to do the right thing instead of disobeying authority. After the long lecture, Amy waited breathlessly to see what Miss Kay was leading up to. Would she be expelled? Thankfully, she wasn't. Instead, she was given some extra duties to perform. She had to get up half an hour early each morning and clean out the downstairs fire grates, and every Saturday night for a month she was to help the chambermaid polish all the silverware.

For the next couple of months, things went smoothly for Amy. There were no more comets or any other once-in-a-lifetime events on the horizon, so she settled in to study once again.

However, in November, just before her fifteenth birthday, Amy was again called into Miss Kay's office. This time, Miss Kay asked her to sit down. She had "difficult" news, she said. Amy and her brothers, Norman and Ernest, who attended a nearby boys' school, were to go home to Ireland at once. Amy's father, David Carmichael, had not given any reason for their sudden return home, but he had said that they would not be returning to school. So in the middle of the school year, Amy packed up her belongings and, along with her two brothers, boarded a train that would take them from the Yorkshire countryside to Liverpool, where they would take a steamboat across the Irish Sea to Ireland and home. Only it wasn't the same home they'd left. Amy's parents and younger brothers and sisters had moved from the old, gray stone country house into the city of Belfast. The move was because of Mr. Carmichael's work. Amy's father and his brother William owned a large flour mill in Millisle. The mill had been in the family for more than one hundred years, but the two brothers had kept it as up-to-date as they possibly could. It was the first mill in the area to have new rollers to grind the wheat, and it was steam powered. It even had gas lighting.

The Carmichael brothers had decided to open another mill nearer Belfast. So the family had moved into a house in College Gardens while the oldest three children were away at boarding school. But things weren't going as well as planned. For the first time in a hundred years, the Carmichaels' flour mills were losing money. It didn't matter how efficiently the brothers ran their two mills. The problem was not the mills; it was new fast steamships. The wheat used in the mills to make the flour came from America. It was shipped to Liverpool, England, and then sent on to Ireland. Once in Ireland, the Carmichael Mills would grind it into flour, which was sold in Ireland and England.

The new fast steamships, however, made it possible to grind the wheat in America and then ship the flour straight to England, where it arrived in good condition and not infested with bugs, as was often the case during long sailboat trips across the Atlantic Ocean from North America. This meant that the Irish mills were having to produce their flour more and more cheaply to compete with American flour, until they were making hardly any profit at all. For the Carmichaels, that meant there was no money for private boarding schools, so Amy and her brothers had been called home.

Amy, though, continued to study music, painting, and singing at a private finishing school in Belfast, which suited her fine. She was glad the whole family was together again. In many ways, Marlborough House had been a lonely place for her, but she never was alone at home, not with six brothers and sisters, and Uncle William's five children, who seemed to visit a lot. There were always enough children around the house to organize into teams for games.

Amy also liked being in the city. She was allowed to explore Belfast on her own. She loved to walk around and look at the huge five-story brick buildings that made up most of the city and stand by the side of the road and watch the horse-drawn trams go by.

One day, after she had been out exploring, Amy walked into the drawing room while her mother and father were having a serious conversation. Her mother looked as if she was about to cry, and her father was shrugging his shoulders and saying, "What can I do? What can I do?" Amy backed out of the room, not wanting to disturb her parents' privacy.

Soon enough, though, she found out what they had been talking about. On top of the money problems created by cheap American flour, Mr. Carmichael had loaned one thousand pounds to a friend to help him get back on his feet after some financial difficulties. But the friend had lost Mr. Carmichael's money, and Mr. Carmichael would not send his friend into bankruptcy by demanding it back. As a result, there wasn't enough money for Amy to continue attending the finishing school. Instead, she began tutoring the younger children at home.

Mr. Carmichael worried continually about money. He spent hours thinking about how he could have done things differently. He worried so much that his health began to suffer, and in April 1885, he came down with pneumonia. Amy, now seventeen years old, nursed him day and night, but he did not recover like a man of fifty-three ought to have, and within several weeks he was dead.

Everything changed for Amy the day her father died. She was suddenly pushed into adulthood. As the oldest daughter, new responsibilities fell to her. It would be her job to care for the younger children. And to stretch out as far as possible what money her father had left, she also helped her mother with the care and cleaning of the house. There was no paying for servants to do those chores anymore.

Despite it all, Amy didn't waste time feeling sorry for herself. She had a job to do, and her mother and brothers and sisters were depending on her. If it meant she would spend the next ten years taking care of her younger siblings, that is what she would do. And she would make it as much fun as she possibly could.

Chapter 3

A Voice from the Fountain

It took a while for things to settle down, but slowly life around the Carmichael house fell into a new pattern. But one thing didn't change. Amy's parents had been strong Christians, and although Mr. Carmichael was now dead, each Sunday Mrs. Carmichael continued to take the children to the Rosemary Street Presbyterian Church. The family walked to church together dressed in their best clothes. On the walk home, Amy and her brothers Norman and Ernest liked to walk ahead of their mother and the other children. It was on one of these walks home after church that something happened that completely changed Amy's life.

It was a cold, dreary day, and Dr. Park, pastor of the Rosemary Street Presbyterian Church, had preached a particularly long sermon. After an hour and a half sitting in the drafty church, the whole Carmichael family was eager to get home to the warmth of the fire in the drawing room fireplace. As usual, Amy, Norman, and Ernest strode out in front. They were winding their way through the streets back to College Gardens when an old beggar woman came staggering out of a side alley. Her clothes were tattered, and her feet were wrapped in strips of rags that were clogged with mud. Slung across her back in an old coal sack was a bundle of sticks. The old woman was doubled over under the weight of the heavy bundle. As the woman stumbled along, Amy and her two brothers stopped and looked at her. Despite their father's money woes, the Carmichael children had grown up with much more money than most people. Yet they had also been taught to help others regardless of whether they were rich or poor. So with a shrug, the three of them walked up beside the old woman. Norman lifted the bundle of sticks from her back while Amy and Ernest each took hold of one of the woman's arms and walked along beside her. The old beggar woman smiled a toothless smile and pointed toward another alley about half a mile farther down the street.

The three Carmichael children had expected to help the old woman to a nearby building. The alley she pointed out was farther away than they'd intended to help her. Nonetheless, they would see her safely there. As they made their way along the street, Amy and Ernest, dressed in their best clothes, guided the old woman in tattered rags, while Norman, also in his Sunday best, followed along behind with the pile of sticks slung across the back of his topcoat. What they hadn't figured on was that at the pace the old woman was walking, other people on their way home from church would catch up with them. But that is exactly what began to happen. One by one, church members stared at the strange sight as they walked by. Amy felt her face getting hotter as each person from church passed them, especially when one woman hurried her children to the other side of the road to avoid the four of them altogether.

Embarrassed, Amy and her brothers kept their heads down, not even looking at each other and hoping no one important came along and saw them. There was a fountain in the center of the road, and trying to take her mind off walking along beside the beggar woman, Amy studied it closely. It was made of blocks of cut stone, and the water sprayed out from three spouts at its center. As she studied it, Amy suddenly stopped. Someone was talking to her. She clearly heard a voice say, "Gold, silver, precious stones, wood, hay, straw...the fire will test what sort of work each one has done. If the work which any man has built on the foundation survives, he will receive a reward."

Amy turned to see who was speaking. There was no one there. But she had heard a voice, plain and clear. Puzzled, she walked on with the old woman on her arm. As she did, something felt very different inside. Amy was no longer embarrassed. In fact, she walked with her head held high for all to see. The trio escorted the old woman to where she wanted to go and then ran to catch up to their mother and the other children to finish the walk home.

After lunch, Amy went to her room. She knelt down by her bed. She knew the words she'd heard at the fountain were from the Bible, and finally she located them in her small, leather-bound edition. The words were from 1 Corinthians, chapter three, verses twelve through fourteen. Amy read them again. *What was their meaning to her?* Amy had known for as long as she could remember that God loved her, but she began to wonder about how knowing He loved her changed the way she acted each day.

After several hours of praying and thinking, Amy finally decided she knew what the words from the verse meant to her. For one thing, she would no longer waste time on things that weren't important in God's eyes. When all the things she'd done in her life were finally judged by God, she wanted them to be found worthwhile. She wanted them to be seen as gold and silver, not hay and stubble. For another thing, she would never again worry about what people thought of her. If what she was doing was pleasing to God, that would be enough for her. If other people, even other Christians, didn't want to walk with beggars, that was their business, but Amy would walk with them, and she would walk proudly.

When she finally came downstairs for dinner, Amy had a new purpose in her heart, a purpose that would lead to some very unusual changes in her life.

Amy had always been kind. As a small girl, she had once visited Belfast with her mother. During the visit, they had stopped at a tearoom for a cup of tea and some scones. As they ate, Amy noticed a grimy little beggar girl with her nose pressed up against the tearoom window. The poor little girl with no food was looking in at the rich little girl who had a plateful. The gaze in the little girl's eyes had affected Amy deeply. When Amy got back home to Millisle, she sat down in front of her nursery fireplace and wrote a promise to the girl:

> When I grow up and money have,
> I know what I will do,
> I'll build a great big lovely place
> For little girls like you.

Amy was also kind to animals. She couldn't stand to see them suffer. Once, on her way to family prayers, she had noticed a mouse drowning in a bucket of water. Without a second thought, she scooped up the mouse and dropped him into her apron pocket. Unfortunately, the mouse had squeaked when her father was praying, and Amy was punished for disrupting the peace. But she had saved a mouse's life, so the punishment was worth it.

But as kind as Amy had been in the past, there was something different about her now. She wasn't going to be kind just because that was the right thing to do. She was going to be kind because God had asked her to be kind to those He loved. Amy's two younger sisters were amazed at the change in her. They called her new attitude "Amy's enthusiasms." And Amy *was* enthusiastic. There was so much to do, so many people she knew God wanted her to love and be kind to.

While Amy wanted to learn more about God, she also wanted to help others learn about Him. On Sunday afternoons she would wander the streets of College Gardens and invite the local children back to the Carmichael house, where she would hold a children's meeting. The children would sing and clap, and Amy would read them Bible stories and tell them how God loved them. While Amy was busy with the children, Mrs. Carmichael made sandwiches and lemonade for them all to enjoy when the meeting was over.

Some of the children who came on Sunday afternoons wanted to know even more about God, so Amy started her "Morning Watch Club." The club met on Saturday mornings, and to every child who wanted to join, Amy gave a blank blue card with gold edges. On the card she had the children write out a pledge that they would spend time every day praying and reading their Bible. When they had signed the pledge card, they gave it back to Amy. Every Saturday morning after that they would meet together and discuss how well they were doing keeping their pledges. Everyone, even Amy's two youngest brothers, looked forward to the Morning Watch Club. Amy seemed to be able to make it so much fun as they talked and learned from each other.

Amy and her friend Eleanor Montgomery also ran a night school for boys. The school met on Monday evenings, and Amy and Eleanor would help the boys who had to work in the factories during the day with their reading and writing. They would finish each night with a short "good night service," during which Amy read from the Bible and prayed. Sometimes Eleanor's father, Dr. Montgomery, would come along and help out. He also volunteered at the Belfast City Mission, and he soon noticed that Amy was far more interested in doing God's work than participating in the normal social activities of eighteen-year-old young women.

Eventually, Dr. Montgomery invited Amy to go with him some Saturday evenings when he visited the slums in Belfast. Amy could think of nothing else she would rather do! And so, on Saturday nights, Amy entered a different world, the world of Belfast's slums, where she was introduced to things she'd never seen before. She had seen beggars on the streets; she'd even helped some of them, but nobody had bothered to tell her just how desperate these people's lives really were or what they would do to stay alive. Another thing Amy discovered in the slums was the smells. There was the smell of rotting vegetable peelings that had been thrown onto the pavement from second-story windows, the smell from makeshift toilets created in doorways or stair entrances, the smell from smoky sod fires that drunken men huddled around in the middle of the street. Amy winced at what she smelled and saw. In her wildest imagination she'd never thought human beings could live this way.

One Saturday evening as Amy and Dr. Montgomery made their way around the slums handing out bread and gospel tracts, a small blue-eyed girl wearing a ragged dress walked up to Amy and started begging for food. As Amy looked down at her, an old woman with her head wrapped in a shawl stepped forward and picked up the girl. As the woman turned to walk away with the child in her arms, Amy gasped. The shawl had fallen from the old woman's face, and the woman was not old at all. She was probably about the same age as Amy. *What kind of life has this woman led to make her back so stooped and her face so worn when she cannot be more than twenty years old?* After they had given out all the bread and tracts, Amy asked Dr. Montgomery the question she'd been pondering.

Dr. Montgomery told her the women were called "shawlies." He went on to explain that shawlies, many of them as young as ten years old, worked twelve hours a day in the linen mills that made Belfast famous. Irish linen, Irish shirts, Irish rope were among the best quality in the world, and yet they were cheap to buy. They were cheap because the girls who worked in the mills were poorly paid for their labor. Most didn't even earn enough money to buy themselves a hat, so they pulled their shawls up over their heads when they went out in the cold, thus the nickname shawlies.

Amy couldn't stop thinking about the shawlies. Something had to be done for them. Slowly she hatched a plan. Why not start holding meetings on Sunday mornings for the shawlies like the one she held for the neighborhood children on Sunday afternoons? She decided the hall at Rosemary Street Presbyterian Church would be a great place to hold her meetings. The church hall had plenty of room, and Amy was sure everyone in the church would love to see it used to reach out to the less fortunate citizens of Belfast.

Amy visited Dr. Park, pastor of the church, and asked him for permission for the shawlie girls to meet on Sunday mornings for Bible study and prayer in the church hall. Whether Dr. Park thought it was a good idea or whether Amy was impossible to turn down is not certain, but the pastor gave his permission for Amy to hold the shawlie meetings in the church hall.

Some members of the congregation were not happy when they discovered that the riffraff of Belfast were using the church hall. Many church folk, even friends who had known the Carmichaels for a long time, couldn't figure out why Amy would want to associate with shawlies, let alone bring them to church. Some wondered whether Amy was aware that shawlies smelled bad and had fleas and lice. What if some of their fleas and lice crawled onto the church furniture? Soon Dr. Park was being regularly visited by church members who urged him to withdraw his permission for Amy to use the church hall for her meetings. Each time, Dr. Park refused. Frustrated by his response, some church members went straight to Amy and told her what they thought about her meetings with the shawlie girls. Amy did not care what they thought. Ever since the day she had heard the voice at the fountain she hadn't cared what anyone thought of her. All she wanted to do was please God and share His love with others.

All her "enthusiasms" and her responsibilities around the house kept Amy very busy. In September 1886, her mother decided that Amy needed a vacation. Amy chose to go to Scotland and stay with an old school friend, Sarah McCullen. While in Scotland, the two girls traveled down to Glasgow for a Keswick meeting. Keswick was actually the name of a place in England, where twelve years before there had been some large, Christian tent meetings. Since that time, the same type of meetings had been held all over the British Isles, and they had become known as Keswick meetings.

Amy had heard a lot about Keswick meetings, and as she sat and listened to the speaker, she expected something wonderful to happen to her. But nothing did. The speaker was interesting, but Amy didn't think anything he said was particularly powerful. Sarah, on the other hand, sat with her eyes wide and sparkling, staring at the preacher and nodding in agreement at everything he said. While Sarah was totally absorbed in the meeting, Amy sat thinking about how tight her shoes felt. Her stomach was rumbling, and she hoped the preacher would finish soon so she could go to lunch. Amy had heard so many wonderful stories of how people had experienced God during Keswick meetings that she felt disappointed. She wondered if she just wasn't getting it, or if people had exaggerated about what they'd experienced in the meetings.

Before she could decide on an answer, the preacher finished his sermon, clapped his Bible shut, and sat down. The chairman of the meeting got up to close the service in prayer. "O Lord," he began. "We know you are able to keep us from falling...."

The words struck Amy like a bolt of lightning. God was able to keep her from falling. Amy's mind focused tightly on that thought. Even after the chairman had finished his prayer and everyone had begun leaving, Amy stayed deep in thought. Finally, Sarah had to pull her to her feet, but even then, Amy did not want to leave. For the first time since walking with the old beggar woman past the fountain, Amy felt as if God had spoken directly to her heart. He would keep her from falling no matter where she went, what she did, or what happened to her while doing it. God would keep her from falling. And if God would keep her from falling, there was nothing she couldn't do. Amy could hardly wait to get back to Belfast. She had plans, big plans for the future.

Chapter 4

Tin Tabernacle

After her experience in Glasgow, Amy arrived back in Ireland with one thought on her mind: She would no longer confine herself to doing what she thought she could do; instead she'd trust God and see what He would do through her.

She threw herself into her work with the shawlies, and before long, the group she'd started two years before had grown to be very big. Every Sunday morning four hundred women and girls crowded into the Rosemary Street Presbyterian Church hall. Of course, many church members continued to complain of being "overrun" by shawlies. They spoke about them as though they were rats.

With so many shawlies coming to her meeting, Amy began to think it might be better for everyone if her shawlie group had its own permanent meeting place. And so, while her two younger sisters, Ethel and Eva, scoured women's journals looking for the latest fashions and discussing what a perfect husband ought to be like, Amy pored over journals about building and engineering. Unlike her sisters and most young women of her era, Amy wasn't interested in marriage. Perhaps she knew it would be a rare man who would let her do what she felt God had called her to do in life. And so she dismissed marriage from her mind and concentrated on her work among the shawlies.

As she flipped through the pages of one particular building journal, her eyes were attracted to an advertisement that contained a drawing of a huge hall made of iron. Beside the drawing was some text that described prefabricated iron buildings that could be built for five hundred pounds. Amy peered at the drawing, trying to imagine what an iron building would look like in real life. Would it be too cold or too noisy? All the buildings in Belfast were made from stone or brick. Would a metal building really work, or was it just a gimmick? She didn't know; her schooling had been in singing and needlework, not engineering.

If her father had still been alive, he could have told her whether the building was soundly engineered and how it would hold up to the damp Belfast climate. Why, if her father were alive and had not lost most of his money on the flour mills, he might well have paid for the building for her. He'd always given generously to Christian activities, building a hall in Millisle that doubled as a school-house and a church. He had even bought a horse and buggy for the church preacher. But her father was dead, and there was precious little Carmichael money left, perhaps enough to keep the family afloat if they were careful, but certainly not enough to buy a new building.

Amy wondered how she might get the money to buy a building like the iron one she'd seen in the building journal. She could always ask other Christians, of course, but she had asked another Christian for money once, a long time ago, and the bad taste of the experience had never left her. She was ten years old and staying with her grand-mother at the time. Her grandmother had been col-lecting money for charity work, and she had suggested that Amy go down to the new house on the corner and ask the owner if he would make a donation. Amy didn't mind doing it; she saw the man at church every Sunday when she stayed with her grandmother. She studied the outside of the man's new house as she knocked on the door. The house had ornate statues in the garden and the very latest trend, a pagoda with wrought-iron trellis work. Surely, Amy thought, someone as rich as this man would be able to spare a lot of money for her grandmother's charity.

When the man came to the door, Amy explained to him the reason for her visit. To her surprise, the man announced gruffly that he could not spare a single penny for her grandmother's charity work. Amy was shocked. The man was rich; he'd had enough money to build himself an expensive house. How could it be that he didn't have a single penny left over? Amy thought about it as she walked back to her grandmother's house, until it finally dawned on her. The man must have had lots of pennies; he just didn't want to give any of them away.

A new idea took root in Amy's ten-year-old mind that day. Real Christian people, she decided, would gladly give money to help others. So why bother to ask people who didn't want to give?

The incident had happened ten years before, but Amy remembered the experience vividly. She still believed that Christian people would gladly give, and she also believed it was better to ask God to steer those people to give money than it was to ask them directly. At the shawlie meeting the following Sunday morning, she shared with the women the idea of having their own building, and they all agreed to pray and ask God to supply the enormous sum of five hundred pounds for the building and a place to put it.

As the eldest daughter, Amy couldn't always escape the duties that came with living in Victorian society. One thing Amy couldn't avoid was "returning calls" with her mother. Returning calls was an elaborate system where upper-class women made appointments to visit each other in their homes. There was no such thing as just dropping by to visit someone. Instead, calling cards had to be left, and specific times to visit were arranged. Amy hated returning calls; they were always the same. The older women would quiz her on any young men she might find interesting or on which of her sisters was learning a new piano piece. Then the hostess would tell Amy about the latest poetry reading she had attended or which young man had paid a call on which young woman. The conversation was so dull, and combined with sitting up straight in an uncomfortable chair balancing a teacup on her lap for an hour or more, Amy found the visits completely boring and time wasting. Still, it was her duty to accompany her mother, so as tiresome as the visits were, she didn't complain.

Occasionally, though, an unsuspecting hostess would ask Amy what else she was doing. That was the opening Amy needed. She would jump right in and begin talking about the work with the shawlies, the Belfast City Mission, and the YWCA, where she also volunteered with great enthusiasm. She didn't like talking about herself, but she loved to talk about what God was doing in people's lives. Often the hostess would slowly steer the conversation back to more "respectable" topics, but every now and then, Amy would find someone who was interested in what she was doing.

One woman who was genuinely interested in Amy's work was Kate Mitchell, the daughter of a wealthy businessman. Kate listened carefully to Amy and asked her intelligent questions. Amy gladly told Kate all about the work she was involved in around the city. She left the Mitchell house feeling as if she'd made a new friend. And she had. Several days later a letter from Kate arrived that contained some astonishing news. Kate Mitchell wanted to pay the entire price of a hall for the shawlie girls. Amy could hardly believe it. She was so excited. She hadn't asked Kate for the money, so she knew it was God who had caused Kate to offer the money. Amy could hardly wait for Sunday morning to come around so she could share the wonderful news with the shawlies.

Next there was the question of where to put the hall. A building that big didn't fit just anywhere. Because her charity work took her all over the city, Amy knew Belfast better than most people. As she thought about where to put the hall, a lot she'd passed on Cambria Street came to mind. The property was part of a large piece of land that belonged to one of the wealthiest mill owners in Belfast. Amy went to visit him and told him about the hall and how she needed some land to build it on. Then she asked him what price he would accept for the land on Cambria Street. She almost laughed out loud when he told her. Had she heard right? The amount the mill owner wanted was about one-tenth of the real value of the land. In fact, the price was so low that the money Kate Mitchell was planning to pay for the building would cover the cost of the land as well. Again God had provided, and again Amy could hardly wait until Sunday morning to tell the shawlies.

Soon an unusual looking iron building that would seat five hundred people was taking shape on the land on Cambria Street. By Christmas it was finished, and on January 2, 1889, it was officially opened by Dr. Park. Amy did not sit on the stage during the opening, preferring to sit in the audience with the shawlies. As usual, she wanted the spotlight not to be on her but to be on what God had done.

Many people came to the opening just to see what an iron building looked like inside. While the building had officially been named The Welcome, most visitors called it the Tin Tabernacle. Amy didn't really care what people called it. What was important was that the shawlies had a place they could call their own. The Welcome was a place where the shawlies could hear the gospel message, meet with other Christian women, encourage each other, and learn new things.

And meet they did. The weekly schedule that was posted on The Welcome door read as follows:

Sunday	4:30 P.M.	Bible Class
Sunday	5:30 P.M.	Sunbeam Band Meeting
Monday	1:20 P.M.	Lunch Hour Meeting
Monday	7:30 P.M.	Singing Practice
Tuesday	7:30 P.M.	Night School
Wednesday	1:20 P.M.	Lunch Prayer Meeting
Wednesday	7:30 P.M.	Girls' Meeting
Thursday	4:00 P.M.	Mothers' Meeting
Thursday	7:30 P.M.	Sewing Club
Friday	1:20 P.M.	Lunch Hour Meeting

First Wednesday of the month: Gospel Meeting. All Welcome.

If finding the money to build the Tin Tabernacle had been a challenge to Amy, finding people to staff it proved much more so. Amy wasn't a person who believed any help was better than no help. Some people offered to help her because they felt sorry for the shawlies. They wouldn't do. Others offered to help because they felt a need in their lives to "do a little charity work." They wouldn't do, either. Amy turned away more help than she accepted. She allowed only those people to help her who would serve the shawlies out of dedication to God. Nothing less was good enough for Amy, who knew that when difficult decisions had to be made she needed godly people around her, not do-gooders.

While the work at The Welcome began to prosper, things at the Carmichael home were not going well financially. Before he died, Mr. Carmichael had invested most of his remaining money so the family could live off the interest. But the investment had gone bad and the money was lost. The Carmichaels no longer had a little money on which to survive; they now had none. Instead of feeling sorry for herself, Mrs. Carmichael trusted that God would work things out, no matter how dark things seemed. She gathered her seven children together and told them the bad news. Then they all knelt down and prayed about the situation and asked God to guide them.

A few days later, Jacob MacGill, an old friend of the Carmichaels, offered Mrs. Carmichael a job overseeing a women's rescue home in the industrial city of Ancoats, on the outskirts of Manchester, England.

He also offered Amy support in starting up a ministry among the mill workers there. After praying about it for a long time, Amy felt she should go with her mother to England, as did her sister Ethel. Norman and Ernest decided to emigrate to North America, while Eva, Walter, and Alfred stayed in Ireland with relatives. Later on, Walter and Alfred also emigrated, one to South Africa and the other to Canada.

With the move to England, Amy would have to leave the shawlies and The Welcome, where she had poured so much of her energy and love. Thankfully, though, Kate Mitchell had been so inspired by Amy's work that she took Amy's place as director of the center. Still, it was very hard for Amy to say good-bye. Yet in her heart she knew it had never really been her work; it had always belonged to God and always would.

Amy stood on the stern of the steamer that was taking her, her mother, and her sister to England and took in everything as the green hills of Ireland faded from view. She didn't know it then, but it was the last time she would ever see her homeland. The ship continued on through the Strangford Lough and pitched and rolled its way across the Irish Sea to Liverpool, England. As sea spray whipped at her face, Amy, still standing on the stern of the ship, prayed that God would open up new opportunities for her to work among the mill workers of Ancoats.

Chapter 5

Out of the Blue

A petite young woman pulled a knitted shawl tightly around her shoulders and braced herself against the chilling wind. She walked northward toward the smoke-belching factories. Nimbly she avoided the huge puddles that stretched across the road. Horse-drawn carriages clattered past, splashing muddy water on her skirt. A bucket of soapy water tipped from a fourth-story window, narrowly missing her as the water splashed onto the cobbled street. The petite young woman was Amy Carmichael, and she had just stepped from her new home.

To anyone passing, Amy looked like just another shawlie, one of the thousands of Irish women who'd come to England to escape poverty only to find more of it. Amy could have lived with her mother and sister in the small cottage they rented just outside of town, but she had wanted to live in the slum. Living in the same place as the people she wanted to help made all the sense in the world to her. In the three months she'd been living there since arriving from Belfast, she had learned many things. For example, she discovered how difficult it was to live without enough sleep. The walls in her room were paper thin, and she could hear every baby cry, every couple argue, every drunken man beat his wife in every room on her floor. But that was nothing compared to the rats and bugs that infested the building. It was hopeless trying to keep them out. For every bug and every rat Amy chased away, more came in to see what all the commotion was about. The pests ferreted through her clothes at night and scurried lightly over her blankets. Amy slept with her sheet pulled tightly around her neck, not wanting to wake up with a rat or roaches crawling inside her bedclothes. While she may have kept the vermin from getting under her blankets, they went wherever else they pleased. She could hear them scuttling across her table during the night, and in the morning she always dropped one of her boots heavily on the floor before lighting the lamp. The loud noise frightened the bugs and rats and sent them scampering into corners and crevices.

The outside of the slimy, moss-covered brick building was not much better than the inside.

Unemployed men hung around the doorway. Sometimes, when they were drunk, they would yell things at Amy or try to grab her. Once a mob of men had followed her. Things were getting ugly before a kindhearted woman who saw what was happening grabbed Amy and pulled her inside, locking the door quickly behind to keep the men out.

Despite all the roaches, rats, and rough men, Amy wanted to live there. She was continually telling the shawlies they could find peace and joy in their lives, and she needed to know for herself that it was possible to live a happy Christian life in the midst of hardship and squalor.

Despite the difficult living conditions, things went well for Amy. After a year living and working in the slum, she was a familiar figure around the factories and mills of Ancoats. Many shawlies and other women from the factories attended her Bible studies and prayer meetings.

All the meetings she was involved in kept Amy very busy, too busy to cook good meals for herself. Perhaps not eating well was part of the reason she got sick, very sick. No one knew the exact name of her illness. In 1890, doctors had no way to diagnose many of the illnesses we know by name today. Often people were said to have "internal weakness" or "acute neuralgia," which could mean anything from stomach cancer to migraine headaches. For many sicknesses there were no cures, apart from a change of climate, good food, and rest. The doctor decided Amy needed all three.

The question for Amy was where to go for rest, good food, and a change of climate. The answer came by way of a family friend, Robert Wilson, who was a wealthy coal mine owner. He had first met the Carmichael family three years before when he had come to Belfast with Hudson Taylor to run a Keswick meeting. In fact, Robert Wilson, together with Canon Hartford-Battersby, the vicar of St. John's Keswick, had founded the Keswick meetings. While Robert Wilson was visiting Belfast, Amy's aunt had invited him to the Carmichael house. During his visit he had become very interested in what everyone in the household was doing. He was especially interested in Amy's work with the shawlies, and every time he returned to Belfast, he made it a point to visit the Carmichaels. Everyone at the Carmichael house looked forward to his coming, and after several visits, the Carmichael children took to calling him "the D.O.M.," which stood for Dear Old Man.

Robert Wilson lived in a large manor house called Broughton Grange, located in the Lake District of England. When he heard that Amy was sick, he invited her to stay at Broughton Grange (the Grange, as it was called by most people). At the Grange, Robert Wilson's cook would make her delicious soups, his housekeeper would nurse her back to health, and the wonderful country air would be just what she needed after the grime of the city. It was a perfect solution, except that Amy wanted so badly to stay with her new shawlie group. But this was not possible; she could barely get out of bed in the morning, and she was eating less and less each day. So she took Robert Wilson up on his kind offer and moved into the Grange.

What a contrast life at the Grange was. Each day a fire was crackling in her bedroom fireplace when she awoke. She had thick, home-churned butter on fluffy scones for morning tea and took long walks in the fields among the sheep or gathered duck eggs from the edge of the pond. Each night the feather eiderdown on her bed was turned down for her. In no time at all, the color began to return to Amy's cheeks.

Of course, Amy being Amy, as soon as she felt a little better, was looking for something to do. And she found plenty. Robert Wilson needed a lot of organizing. As chairman of the Keswick Convention, he had numerous responsibilities arranging Keswick meetings all over the British Isles. He also had many letters to write. Amy took over much of the letter writing for him. Also, Robert Wilson often needed to entertain important people, and Amy made a wonderful hostess. She especially liked it when Hudson Taylor or George Mueller came to visit. These men had so many amazing stories to tell of how God had changed people's lives. And of course, wherever Amy went, she found children. Broughton Grange was no exception. Within a few weeks she had a group of local girls from Broughton Village coming to the Grange for a Bible study on Saturday afternoons. She held the Bible study in the library, and when it was over, the girls had milk and gingerbread on the lawn terrace. Then they fanned out through the garden, skipping and giggling as they explored. They teased the kittens, admired the peacocks, raced the dogs, and rode the ponies.

Seeing the young girls enjoying themselves in the garden made Amy very happy, but not Robert Wilson's two sons, George and William, who also lived at the Grange. Their mother had died the same year as Amy's father, and their only sister, Rachel, had died before that. Both of them were now middle-aged men, and neither had married. And that was the way they liked things. To them, the Grange was a man's place. It was a place for hunting and fishing and discussing politics. Until Amy had arrived, it was a quiet, dignified place, and the brothers were unhappy to see it overrun with females. They referred to it as an "invasion," and they had no intention of letting Amy feel completely at home at the Grange. Despite their best efforts to make Amy feel unwelcome, their father grew to rely on her. In fact, he began to treat Amy as though she were his own daughter. He spent many hours discussing Christian things with her and encouraging her in her dedication to God.

One day, after Amy had been at the Grange for about three months, Robert Wilson asked her to stay on once she was completely well and continue to be the hostess for his home and ministry. At first Amy struggled with the idea. Her heart was in the slums with the shawlies, but as she prayed about it, a strange peace came over her. She knew that for some reason she could not yet understand, God wanted her to live at Broughton Grange.

Amy kept busy around the Grange. Robert Wilson's two sons dutifully invited her to go along with them to a Scripture Union Bible study they attended each Tuesday night in the village. Amy made such an impact on the group that she was asked to lead all their meetings, which did not sit well with George and William. Amy also visited the surrounding villages, holding meetings and sharing the gospel message with all who cared to listen. She took to writing and had her first short story published. The story, *Fightin' Sall*, was about how God had changed the life of one of the shawlies in Belfast. Amy also helped Robert Wilson arrange all the Keswick meetings held in the British Isles. On top of that, she regularly visited her mother at the rescue mission and helped her there.

A full and happy year at the Grange quickly passed for Amy. Then one day, out of the blue, something she had heard several years before strangely came to mind. Hudson Taylor from the China Inland Mission had been the speaker at the first Keswick meeting in Belfast, and Amy had gone to hear him speak. During the meeting, Taylor told the audience about the four thousand Chinese who died every hour without ever having heard the gospel message. Amy had taken it all in, but it had remained buried in her mind until one afternoon

five years later at the Grange, when she found herself thinking about Hudson Taylor's message. In
fact, she couldn't seem to get the thought out of her
mind, and she didn't quite know what to do with it.
In early January 1892, she decided to spend some
time praying about it. She had been praying for
only a few minutes when the hair on the back of her
neck stood on end. She opened her eyes and looked
around. Just as she'd heard at the fountain back in
Belfast, she heard a voice say, "Go ye." Amy knew
these were the first words to a verse in the Bible.
She knew the verse by heart: "Go ye into all the
world and preach the gospel."

Amy spent a restless night thinking about what
the verse could mean to her. She had expected to be
Robert Wilson's assistant until he died, whenever
that might be. Did God now want her to leave
Robert Wilson after he'd become so dependent on
her? And what about all the work she had been
doing for the Keswick meetings? Was she supposed
to leave all of that as well? And then there was her
mother, who depended on Amy to help her make
family decisions. What would happen to her
mother if she left? Amy tossed and turned, but by
the morning she had come to a conclusion. God had
said to her, "Go," and whatever the cost, that was
what she would do.

That morning, she sat at her desk overlooking
the picturesque English countryside and began writing a letter to her mother. But somehow she couldn't
finish it. It was too painful imagining her mother

reading the letter, so Amy put it aside. The next day she picked the letter up again and struggled through it. With a heavy heart, she mailed it.

Next, she turned her attention to telling Robert Wilson she would be leaving.

Amy trembled as she told him about her new direction. Robert Wilson had been like a father to her, and it was hard to think she might be disappointing him. But sad as he was to lose her, he understood her determination to obey God. Surprisingly, though, his two sons were not as understanding. Without admitting it, they had become very used to having Amy around the house. She had made the house come alive with music and laughter, and they liked that. They also liked the stream of unconventional visitors Amy brought to the Grange. Now they wondered how she could possibly think of leaving. Not only were the Wilson brothers against Amy's leaving, so were the leaders of the Keswick Convention. Things had run so smoothly at the Grange with Amy there, and they wondered how Robert Wilson would function without her.

It all made Amy's head swirl. She wondered why following God wasn't easier and why other Christians found it so hard to understand what she wanted to do. But other Christians' not understanding wasn't going stop her. God had told her to go, but where? It took several months before Amy settled that question. She would follow Hudson Taylor to China.

In early August 1892, Robert Wilson and Amy
set off for London, where Amy could apply to join
the China Inland Mission. It was just a formality.
Hudson Taylor already knew Amy quite well and
knew she would be a useful addition to any mission. Amy met with Miss Soltau, who screened the
women who applied to join the China Inland
Mission. Miss Soltau gave Amy some forms to fill
out. At the top of the first form was a space for
Amy's name. "You had better write Amy *Wilson*
Carmichael there so that everyone will know you
have meant as much to me as any daughter could,"
Robert Wilson instructed her. Amy wrote in the
name just the way he had said, and from then on,
that was the name she went by.

Amy made a positive impression on Miss Soltau,
and before she knew it, she'd been accepted as a
missionary. Miss Soltau whisked her around
London outfitting her for China. She had obviously
done it many times before and knew which stores
to go to and exactly how much would fit into a tin
sea chest. Amy was soon outfitted and ready to go.

Amy stayed at the China Inland Mission house
in London while she waited for several other
women to arrive so they could all travel as a group
to China. While there, she began learning some
Chinese. She couldn't have been more ready to go,
nor could the China Inland Mission have been
more ready to send her. Or so it seemed. There was
just the matter of her medical history. Amy looked
strong and healthy at a glance, but her illness in the

slums of Ancoats had left her body weakened. The doctor who gave her a physical before she was to depart for China did not like what he saw. In his opinion, there was no way Amy could stand up to the illnesses she would be exposed to in China. Any of the diseases that flourished in the tropics, such as dengue fever, typhoid, and yellow fever, would kill her. The doctor would not permit Amy to go to China as a missionary with the China Inland Mission, and his word was final.

In a daze, Amy hired a buggy to take her and her tin sea chest back to Broughton Grange. She didn't know what else to do. Of course, Robert Wilson was delighted to see her return. Amy fit right back into life at the Grange, but in her heart she was restless. What had gone wrong? Why had she felt God call her to go to China and gone through all the agony of saying good-bye to her mother and Robert Wilson, only to be turned down by a doctor? She didn't understand. But she wasn't about to give up, either. One thing she knew for sure as she looked at the tin sea chest shoved in the corner of her room. God had said, "Go," and she would go somewhere, and soon.

Chapter 6

Laughing in the Rain

Four months after arriving back at the Grange Amy felt "the call," as she put it, to Japan. But what would she do there? She didn't know a single person in Japan or anyone connected with missionary work there. Robert Wilson, of course, knew missionaries all over the world. When Amy told him she felt called to Japan, Barclay Buxton came immediately to his mind. Buxton was a missionary sent out by the Church Missionary Society, the missionary arm of the Church of England. He was the leader of a group called the Japanese Evangelistic Band. The group was made up of missionaries from a number of denominations, and Robert Wilson knew they would welcome a young, female, Irish Presbyterian missionary.

After her rejection by the China Inland Mission and her return to Broughton Grange, Robert Wilson had thought Amy would settle down. It had been so good to have her back, but now she wanted to leave again. The letter to Barclay Buxton asking whether there was a place for Amy on his team was not easy for Robert Wilson to write. He also worried about Amy's health. If she wasn't healthy enough to go to China, how was it she thought herself healthy enough to go to Japan? It made no sense to him. Yet he knew Amy believed God had told her to go, and she was a very determined person. So, although he didn't want to lose her again, he did all he could to help her with her plans.

Certain that God had called her to Japan, Amy didn't bother to wait for a reply from Barclay Buxton. Three women from the China Inland Mission were sailing to Shanghai in early March, and Amy planned to travel with them. In Shanghai she would transfer to another ship for the journey to Japan. She had Robert Wilson ask Barclay Buxton to send his reply to Shanghai so it would be waiting for Amy when she arrived.

On March 3, 1892, along with her tin sea trunk, Amy boarded the SS *Valetta* at Tilbury, on the river Thames near London. Amy would have preferred to climb the gangway, wave good-bye, and head out to sea, but it wasn't that easy. Saying good-bye for an extended sea voyage was long and drawn out. Many people who left on such voyages never returned. There were shipwrecks, diseases, and disasters waiting in the Far East, and those who were staying at home often acted as though they were at a funeral rather than a farewell. Amy had said a tearful good-bye to her mother in Manchester, but Robert Wilson had insisted on escorting her all the way to the dock. Amy stood on the deck of the *Valetta* and waved good-bye to him. Tears streamed down her cheeks as those on the dock sang Keswick hymns to her and the other three missionary women aboard. As the ship began to drift from the dock, Amy was both sad and relieved as Robert Wilson began to fade from view. It was hard leaving him, not knowing whether she would ever see him again.

As the *Valetta* rounded the end of the dock and began to drift with the current on the river Thames, there was Robert Wilson again. He had quickly hiked along the dock to catch one last look at his beloved Amy. The *Valetta* passed so close to where he was standing that he and Amy could call to each other. They encouraged each other with Bible verses, and then, when Amy thought she could bear it no more, the ship finally pulled out into the main channel of the river, and for the last time, Robert Wilson became a tiny waving speck on the dock.

Amy had done it. She had left behind her mother and her adopted father to follow God's leading. Later in life, she said it was the most difficult thing she had ever had to do.

Life aboard the SS *Valetta* settled into a pattern. Amy was seasick, but not anywhere near as seasick as many of the other passengers. As usual, she soon set to work organizing things. Within a week, there were morning Bible readings on the poop deck and Sunday services in the saloon. Amy and one of the China Inland Mission women began a Bible study aboard ship that attracted an odd assortment of passengers and crew: a high-class Indian man searching for "truth," a Chinese woman from Sowtow, a poor Indian man who had sold himself as a slave to work in the sugar plantations in the West Indies, and a Chinese nanny.

As the *Valetta* entered the Mediterranean Sea and steamed along the north coast of Africa, Amy found other opportunities to talk to passengers and crew members about the gospel message. At Port Said, the ship headed south through the one-hundred-and-one-mile-long Suez Canal. Then it steamed through the Red Sea and on into the Indian Ocean. Everyone was glad when the *Valetta* finally reached Colombo, Ceylon. Amy and the three other women headed for Shanghai had to spend several days in Colombo before boarding another ship for the second leg of their journey. Amy spent her time visiting missionaries she'd heard about through her Keswick connections.

Finally, Amy boarded the SS *Sutlej* bound for Shanghai. Unlike the *Valetta*, the *Sutlej* was a nightmare, with rats and cockroaches infesting the ship. For Amy it brought back memories of living in the slums of Ancoats. But instead of complaining about the condition of the ship, Amy found a large piece of cardboard, on which she wrote the words "In Everything Give Thanks." She placed the cardboard by her bunk where she could read it before she went to sleep every night.

Amy must have lived out what she had written, because she made a big impact on the captain during the voyage. He told her he had never seen a passenger who had such a positive attitude amid the poor conditions on his ship. During the trip he questioned Amy over and over about her faith, until he finally announced he wanted to become a Christian just like her. Of course, Amy was delighted, and more so when he asked her to write out some Bible verses on cardboard so he could stick them on the walls of his cabin. It was his way of announcing to the whole crew he was now a Christian.

The captain's conversion to Christianity was the only bright spot of the voyage. Amy was grateful when the ship finally steamed up the Yangtze River and then the Huangpu River and docked at Shanghai, where she stayed with missionaries from the China Inland Mission. In Shanghai, a letter was waiting for her from Barclay Buxton. Yes, the letter informed her, the Japanese Evangelistic Band had a place for her, and one of their missionaries would meet her when she arrived at the port of Shimonoseki in southern Japan.

After a short stay in Shanghai, Amy boarded the SS *Yokohama Maru* for the last leg of her trip to Japan. During the voyage, the ship ran into a fierce typhoon. When she couldn't dock at Shimonoseki because of the storm, her passengers were loaded onto a tugboat for a rough ride ashore.

Finally, as the typhoon began to subside, Amy set foot on Japanese soil. She had safely made it halfway around the world. Feeling weak from five days of constant seasickness, she plunked herself down on her tin sea trunk and looked around for the missionary who was supposed to be meeting her.

Through the pouring rain, Amy noticed light brown faces staring at her. She didn't blame the people for staring. She realized she must look quite a sight. Her felt hat was completely soaked, and she could feel it flopping down to her ears. The rain formed rivulets that dripped off her hat and ran down her dress. Every inch of her, all the way to her starched petticoat, was wet.

The missionary who was supposed to meet her was not there. Feeling a little panicked, Amy began to look around for any white face. There wasn't one. Over the howling wind she yelled, "Does anyone speak English?" There were a few giggles from those around her, but no reply—at least no reply she could understand. She tried again. "My name is Amy Carmichael, can anyone help me?" Still no answer. Suddenly Amy saw the humor in the situation. She had come halfway around the world and was now stuck on a dock in Japan in the midst of a typhoon with not the slightest idea of what to do next. She started to laugh. And the more she thought about it, the more she laughed, until tears of laughter joined the raindrops that cascaded down her cheeks.

When she finally finished laughing, two Japanese men stepped forward and motioned for her to stand up. They hooked ropes under the handles of her trunk and hung the trunk on a bamboo pole between them. They motioned for her to follow them. Amy followed as the two men talked to each other in short, fast sentences. The men led the way along the dock, around a corner, and into a street. Amy couldn't see the end of the street; the rain was still too heavy. Besides, she had to concentrate hard to avoid the huge puddles and ruts in the road. The trio trudged on for a few hundred yards until the men ducked into a building. Amy followed. Finally, the shorter of the two men beckoned for her to sit on a woven grass mat in a room inside the building. As she did so, the men bowed and left the room. Amy was alone, sitting cross-legged on a mat. It wasn't particularly comfortable, but at least she was out of the rain. She looked around the room. The walls were made with panels of very thin paper, and there was not a piece of furniture to be seen. Amy was aware her clothes were making a big puddle on the mat. She hoped it wouldn't be difficult to mop up.

Amy sat for nearly half an hour before one of the men reappeared and again motioned for her to follow. The man led Amy outside to a rickshaw, or *kuruma* as it was called in Japan. She'd seen the two-wheeled carts pulled by a "driver" in Shanghai, but she had no idea how uncomfortable they were to ride in. Every bone in her body seemed to jolt with each turn of the huge wheels. The wind whipped at her skirt, and she pulled her soaked shawl tightly around her as if it were actually offering some protection from the storm.

Eventually, the *kuruma* stopped outside a house, and the driver lowered its handles and then lifted Amy's sea trunk from between the back axles. Amy had no idea where she was, but she figured this was where she was supposed to get off. When she'd climbed out of the *kuruma*, the driver bowed to her, picked up the cart's handles, and trotted off into the rain.

Amy knocked loudly on the door of the house. Much to her relief, a white man opened it. The man stood stunned for a moment at the small, wet stranger standing in his doorway in the middle of a typhoon. He invited Amy in and offered her some tea. Thankfully, he spoke English, though with an American accent. Over a cup of steaming hot tea, Amy's story tumbled out, and soon her host was chuckling away. The story got funnier and funnier as she told it, until they were both laughing so hard Amy's sides ached. By the time she had finished her story, Amy had made a new friend in the American trader. The trader explained to her that he knew where two missionaries lived, and although he did not know their names, he was reasonably sure they were the ones Amy was meant to stay with. If not, he was certain they would know where she belonged. After several more cups of tea, the trader flagged down another *kuruma* for Amy. He gave a volley of instructions to the driver in Japanese, and then Amy was off again. This time she knew where she was going.

When Amy arrived at the missionary house, she found that the people there were indeed the missionaries who were expecting her. But they were also expecting the missionary who had been sent from a mission station in the country to meet Amy. He hadn't yet arrived, which explained why there was no one to meet Amy at the dock. The other missionaries concluded that the typhoon had held him up and he would get to Shimonoseki as soon as he could. Still, his not being there to meet Amy had given her the opportunity to learn something on her very first day on the mission field: God could make things work out, even when things seemed to be going wrong. Amy thought of the men who had carried her trunk and hired the *kuruma*. She supposed they had paid the driver to take her to the trader, but she had no way of ever finding them again to thank them. And the trader had done the same thing. Amy had been at the mercy of God and the kindness of strangers, and she had been helped every step of the way.

Amy was glad to finally change into some dry clothes. She had been drenched for about six hours since leaving the SS *Yokohama Maru*. She enjoyed a wonderful meal with the other missionaries before she headed to bed. Before going to sleep, she propped herself up in bed and wrote a few lines in her journal about her first day in Japan. She ended it with, "Of all funny experiences, this morning's was the funniest."

The next day, though, Amy learned something that both surprised and upset her. The weather was gray, but not raining, and Amy was glad to be able to get out of the house. She and one of the missionary women she was staying with went for a walk along the beach. They talked about what Amy could expect on the mission field. Amy remarked that no matter what happened among the unconverted, it would be wonderful to always be able to count on the support of other missionaries. The woman stopped and turned to Amy. With a look of total shock on her face she said, "You don't mean to say you think all missionaries *love* one another?" Then she laughed a wait-until-you-find-out kind of laugh.

Amy was dumbfounded. Of course, she believed other missionaries loved one another. It was Jesus Himself who told Christians to love one another. So what did this woman mean? Did she really mean Christian missionaries were no closer to following God's commands than non-Christians? That could not be. Amy wouldn't believe it. That night she prayed for a long time before going to sleep. "Lord, help me to always love other people as You love us. Show me how to love even Christians who do not love me back," she prayed. She would get plenty of practice at doing that in the next fifteen months!

Chapter 7

Enough of English Clothing

It was May 1, 1893, when Amy arrived at the ancient town of Matsuye, her final destination in Japan. She was welcomed by Barclay Buxton and the other missionaries who made up the Japanese Evangelistic Band. Amy was glad to meet them all. She was also thankful for her room at the Buxton house that looked out on snowcapped mountains. The three small Buxton boys were soon trailing around after her.

For her first three months in Matsuye, Amy lived in two worlds. One was the English world within the Buxtons' home. Barclay Buxton was a man with social standing and family money. So rather than leave his three sons in England, as many missionaries of the time did, he brought them and their governess to Japan. As a result, the family kept a schedule very similar to that of any other upper-class Victorian family. Breakfast was at seven-thirty, followed by morning prayers. Then it was school with the governess for the boys and language study for Amy. This was followed by morning tea and more study before a huge hot lunch was served. Much of the food served at the Buxtons' was imported from England, so the meals Amy ate in Matsuye were almost identical to those served at Broughton Grange, complete with condensed milk, canned meat, and English tea.

The missionaries in the Japanese Evangelistic Band continued to wear English clothing, except on Sundays, when they made some exceptions. Because Japanese people always took off their shoes and hats before going indoors, the Evangelistic Band did the same when they went to church. For many of the Victorian woman in their ranks, being seen in public in bare feet was very embarrassing; the women felt half-naked. Nonetheless, they didn't want to offend the Japanese Christians and so persevered, regardless of how they felt.

Outside the Buxton home and the Japanese Evangelistic Band, though, everything was completely foreign. Amy could walk all day and never hear a word of English spoken or see English words written. And the food she ate while out visiting was very different. She never ceased to be amazed at the things that went into Japanese soup, like seaweed, lily roots, and sea slugs, to name a few.

It didn't take long before Amy became frustrated at not being able to communicate more easily outside the Buxton home. Amy worked hard at her language study, but it was slow, tedious work. In typical style, Amy didn't want to wait until she had learned the language before starting to tell people about the gospel message. She needed a means to start talking to the Japanese people right away. She spoke to Barclay Buxton about the situation every morning at breakfast until he finally arranged for her to have her own personal interpreter and Japanese teacher. Her name was Misaki San. Misaki San was a Christian and a good interpreter, who explained many things to Amy about Japanese life and culture and Buddhist beliefs.

As the two women spent time together, Amy studied Misaki San's dress, a kimono—a beautiful floor-length dress. The kimono was tied at the waist with a huge sash, which Misaki San called an obi. On her feet Misaki San wore socks and wooden shoes that were kept about an inch from the ground by two crosspieces on the bottom. Misaki San wore her hair in a bun, but she did not wear a hat.

Amy compared Misaki San's dress to her own. She wore layers of fabric, three white petticoats, a bonnet tied too tightly under her chin, stockings, and laced-up shoes. Amy came to the conclusion that the kimono Misaki San was wearing would be much more comfortable, cheaper to replace, and easier to get around in without causing a scene. Amy began to think she ought to start wearing a kimono.

She was still thinking about it one bitterly cold day when she and Misaki San visited an old woman. Amy was wearing her thick woolen coat and fur gloves. The old Japanese woman tried hard to concentrate on the gospel message Amy and Misaki San were sharing with her, but Amy could tell she was having a hard time keeping her mind on what they were saying. Suddenly, the old woman reached out and touched Amy's hands. She motioned for Amy to take off her gloves, which she did. For the next few minutes the old woman studied the gloves, turning them over and over in her hands before trying them on. Amy and Misaki San never managed to get the old woman's attention back on the gospel message they were sharing.

Afterward, Amy strode back to the Buxton house with a determined look on her face. She'd had enough of English clothing! She was in Japan, halfway around the world from England, and she should be wearing Japanese clothes. Amy chided herself as she walked. If she'd been wearing a kimono, the old woman would still be listening to the gospel message. If her English clothes distracted even one Japanese person from hearing the gospel message, then she didn't want to wear them.

Thankfully, Barclay Buxton could see Amy's point, and Amy became the first member of the Japanese Evangelistic Band to wear native dress. She chose a blue kimono with light green trim. Blue was Amy's favorite color. Amy had the words "God is Love" embroidered in Japanese down the kimono's outside facings. The kimono was very comfortable, and when Amy pulled her dark brown hair back in the same style the Japanese women wore, at a distance it was hard to tell her apart from the other women. The only problem was the shoes. No matter how hard she tried, Amy couldn't get used to teetering on the wooden platform shoes. She could not seem to keep her balance. She decided to wear plain black slippers, which blended easily with her native dress and were easy to slip off and on when entering and leaving a house.

Amy quickly discovered that Japanese people in the streets took almost no notice of her when she was wearing a kimono. What a relief it was to be able to go out and not be stared at by everyone. One afternoon, Amy went out for a walk by herself. She had learned enough Japanese to be able to carry on short conversations. Normally, though, Amy preferred to talk to children because she felt less embarrassed if she made a mistake in front of them. After walking for a while, she stopped in front of a house to talk to a small girl about five years old. Amy asked her if she knew about God and that He loved her. The little girl nodded excitedly. "Yes," she replied. "I'm going to the magic lantern picture show tonight. That is where the foreigners will show their God."

The little girl smiled as she skipped off down the street. Amy gazed after her, trying to grasp what she'd just heard. Buddhism is a religion of many gods and many statues of gods. Buddhists often believe the statue itself is a god and not just an image of a god. Amy wondered whether the small girl thought the pictures of Jesus many missionaries used were actually God. Was God just a picture to the girl? Amy walked home slowly, troubled by what the little girl had said. How could she make Japanese people understand that a picture of Jesus was not a god and contained no magical powers. It was just a picture and could not talk to them or love them. Amy liked pictures of Jesus; she had several hanging in her room. But she wasn't a Buddhist. She knew the pictures were merely representations of what Jesus may have looked like. She didn't worship the pictures as God. But how were Japanese people raised in Buddhism to know they were just pictures and had no power?

By the time Amy reached the Buxton house, she'd made another decision. She would no longer use pictures of Jesus. Even though pictures of Jesus often helped missionaries explain the gospel message, especially when they did not know the language very well, Amy decided it was not worth using them and risking a misunderstanding about who God really was.

She didn't make a big fuss about her decision not to use pictures to help communicate the gospel, but the other missionaries soon noticed she no longer took her picture kit with her. When they asked why, Amy told them as plainly as she could, and many of them understood what she was saying. Within weeks of Amy's meeting the little girl, many of the missionaries in the Japanese Evangelistic Band had put away their picture kits and were describing their Bible stories to the people instead. That way, Buddhist listeners would not get confused and think the missionaries were "showing them their God."

By August, Amy had been in Japan for three months, and she was more than ready to join the other missionaries for a conference in a town called Arima. She had a wonderful time at the conference, which reminded her of the Keswick meetings back in the British Isles. It was also a great opportunity to meet many other missionaries working in Japan. But in the midst of all the people and activity, Amy felt lonely. She had made many friends since arriving in Japan, but as she watched Barclay Buxton and his wife together, she longed for a close relationship like they had. She began wondering whether she ought to marry. Having a husband and perhaps even children on the mission field would make life a lot less lonely.

The more she thought about it, the more Amy began to fear growing old and being alone. Some of her brothers and sisters had married, so why shouldn't she? But she could find no peace inside about the whole issue, so she went to a cave near Arima to pray about it. After several hours in the cave praying about how lonely she felt and asking God whether she should marry, she felt a great peace come over her. In her heart she heard a voice speak and say, "None of those who trust Me shall be lonely."

Amy thanked God for His assurance and climbed out of the cave. She had her answer. She knew she would never marry or have children of her own. But God had promised her she would never be alone, either. If at that moment Amy could have seen the enormous number of children who would call her Mother or the number of missionaries who would love her and were loved back by her in later years, she would have laughed out loud. The one thing Amy Carmichael would never be accused of was being lonely!

Another three months passed, until in November Amy felt she should make a missionary journey. She talked it over with Barclay Buxton, and it was decided she and Misaki San should visit the village of Hirose. Hirose was one of the bigger villages in the area, but it was almost completely Buddhist. There were only nine known Christians living there. Before setting out for the village, Amy and Misaki San spent a day praying about their trip. By the end of the day, Amy felt that God had promised one convert as a result of their trip.

The Christians in Hirose had invited their friends to come hear Amy speak. One Buddhist woman showed up. She was a young silk weaver, and she had given up a day's pay to come and hear about the new God. By the end of the night, she had become a Christian. Amy had the one convert she believed God had promised.

Four weeks later, Amy felt she should make a return trip to Hirose, so she and Misaki San spent another day in prayer. This time Amy felt God promise that there would be two converts as a result of the trip. She shared the news eagerly with Misaki San, and the two of them prayed further about it as they rode in their *kuruma* to Hirose. Sure enough, the silk weaver who had become a Christian four weeks before had shared her new faith with a coworker, who also wanted to become a Christian. Later in the day, Amy talked to an old woman who wanted to become a Christian, too. It was amazing. The Christian population of Hirose had gone from nine to twelve in only a month. Of course, the local Christians were excited and wanted Amy to come back again soon.

Two weeks later, Amy was back. This time she felt that God had promised four converts during her trip. On her arrival, Amy held the same type of meeting she'd held on her previous two visits, but this time there was hardly anyone there to listen. The weather was too cold for most people to come out to a meeting. Still, Amy believed there would be four new Christians in Hirose before she left. She simply had to find who they were.

Meanwhile, the other Christians in town were thinking that Amy had put off Buddhists from becoming Christians on her previous visit by making the gospel too difficult. Amy had told the silk weavers who had become Christians to burn their idols. The other Christians believed that Amy did not understand their culture and that there was nothing wrong with a Christian also having idols in the house. The idols didn't do any harm, and telling Buddhists to burn them made it too difficult for them to become Christians. The others told Amy this, hoping she would see the wisdom of what they said, but she didn't. She believed all idols had to go, and she would tell that to anyone who asked.

The Japanese Christians sighed. Now no one would be interested in what Amy had to say. Still, halfheartedly, they supported her meetings. But as they had thought, no one present seemed interested in the message that Amy came to share. Everyone sat and stared blankly at Amy, who soon realized she wasn't getting through to anyone at all. Just as she was beginning to get discouraged, the room went completely silent, and then a voice spoke. It was the voice of a woman seated in the corner by the door. "I want to believe," she said.

Amy dismissed the meeting and began talking to the woman. When the woman's son came into the room, instead of interrupting, he stood and listened. By the time Amy had finished talking to his mother, the son too was ready to become a Christian. Amy was thrilled. A mother and a son would be able to support each other in their new faith. Amy introduced them to the other Japanese Christians before setting off back to her room for the night. On the way there, she and Misaki San stopped to tell one of the local Christians who had not been at the meeting the good news. When they entered the man's house, he looked relieved. "I am so glad you came," he said. "I have a guest here who wants to know how to find the way to God."

Amy talked with the guest, and before long, she had her third convert. But what about the fourth one? By now it was very cold and very dark, and nearly all the Christians in Hirose had found their way to the house where Amy and Misaki San were. Amy asked them if they knew of anyone else who was interested in becoming a Christian. One man nodded. "My wife is," he said. "She wants to become a 'Jesus person,' but she is out of town and will not be back for a week."

Amy was puzzled. She was sure God had told her there would be four converts in the village during her visit. But how could this man's wife be one of them if she wasn't even in town?

Every time Amy awoke during the night, she prayed that in the morning God would lead her to the fourth person who wanted to become a Christian. At first light, a servant knocked on Amy's door with an urgent message. The man's wife had returned home unexpectedly, and she wanted to talk with Amy. Sure enough, she told Amy of her desire to become a Christian. Amy was overcome with joy. God had promised her there would be four converts, and sure enough, there were! What more could she ask for on her twenty-sixth birthday?

After Christmas, Amy was ready to make yet another trip to Hirose. This time she was sure God had promised there would be eight converts. When she told this to the Christians at Hirose, they were not at all happy. Eight was a huge number of converts to believe God for. What if there were not eight converts? Had Amy thought about that? They would all look foolish. They told Amy it was better to pray for God's blessing on the meetings instead of stirring people up with actual numbers. But Amy was undeterred. She believed that God had promised eight converts, and in the end, the other Christians agreed to believe with her for that number. It was a good thing they did, because there were indeed eight new Christian converts after Amy's meeting. The Christian population of Hirose had tripled since Amy had started holding her meetings.

Once again, Amy left Hirose with excitement in her heart over all the new converts. Over the next few months she made several more trips to the village. For some reason, though, on each of those trips, God did not promise her that a particular number of people would become Christians. Amy explained it later by saying that God makes every blade of grass unique and He makes every situation unique as well.

There was one part of Amy's trips to Hirose that she did not like to talk about: her health. After each trip she was more exhausted than she had been after the previous trip. Sometimes she would have to stay in bed for a full week with terrible headaches, unable to open the drapes because of the glare of the winter sun.

As Amy lay in bed, she had many questions. Was her body going to betray her as it had in Ancoats?

Was the China Inland Mission doctor right? Did she not have the strength to be a missionary? What if her sickness got worse? Should she go home, or should she stay and be a burden on other missionaries? These were not easy questions to answer, but as Amy found herself spending more and more time in her darkened room, she knew she would have to answer them soon.

Chapter 8

Get the Head out of Japan

The fainting was what finally did it. Amy had fainted only once before, back in Ireland when she'd held her younger brother Albert still while the doctor sewed up a gash in his arm. But in Imichi, the Japanese village she was visiting, she had fainted again. She had been out cold with no good excuse. One minute she was talking to several of the local Christians about the evening service where she was to speak, and the next minute she was lying flat on the floor. Kimono hems and the clacking of wooden shoes quickly surrounded her as some Japanese women placed damp towels on her forehead and tried to lift her up off the cold floor. Amy was shocked by what had happened. Even feeling as weak as she had in the past few months, she was supposed to be the strong one. After all, she had once told someone that fainting was nothing more than "weak-minded nonsense!"

Amy scrambled to her feet and apologized to everyone. Several concerned people suggested she call off the meeting, but Amy would not hear of it. She was the scheduled speaker, and speak she would. It turned out to be a long service, and although Amy made it through without fainting again, she paid a price for it. That church service was the last one she ever held in Japan.

When she got back to Matsuye, Barclay Buxton sent for a doctor right away. The doctor's diagnosis was "Japanese head," a rather vague catchall diagnosis for headaches, weakness, and dizziness. There was only one solution for Japanese head: Get the head out of Japan!

The thing Amy dreaded most had happened. Her body was not nearly as strong as her spirit. Barclay Buxton suggested it might be best for her to recuperate at Chefoo on the coast of China. The China Inland Mission had a house there for sick missionaries, and he was sure they would allow Amy to make use of it as well. There seemed to be no other course of action for her to take. After only fifteen months in Japan, Amy said a sad farewell to the country and the missionaries she'd worked with and boarded a steamer for China. She was on her way to throw herself on the mercy of a mission that had rejected her for health reasons. It was humbling for Amy, and she hoped it would not be long before she was better and able to continue her mission work.

After a tedious voyage, Amy finally arrived in Shanghai, where she was met by some women from the China Inland Mission. The women had bad news for her. The house in Chefoo was already filled to overflowing with sick missionaries, and there was no room for Amy. The women offered to let Amy stay with them in Shanghai, and Amy gratefully accepted. After a week of complete rest, she began to feel well enough to think again and, of course, to pray. She asked God what to do next, and seemingly from nowhere came the very distinct impression that she should go to Colombo, Ceylon.

The idea left Amy feeling weak again. Ceylon! How would that be any different from Japan? And what would the Keswick people back in England who supported her think? From the outside she looked like a sick woman touring Asia at her supporters' expense. Would God ever let her settle in one place, or was she going to spend a year here and a year there for the rest of her life?

While Amy didn't have any answers, and weak as she felt, she knew as well as she knew her own name she was supposed to go to Ceylon. So she paid out ten pounds for a ticket, and on July 28, 1894, she boarded another ship, this time bound for Colombo.

Once again, she was met by kind missionaries, who took her to their station and nursed her. Amy wrote to Robert Wilson and to her mother, explaining how she had ended up in Ceylon. Mrs. Carmichael wrote back and suggested Amy might consider coming home. Home! Amy would not hear of it. Her health was improving in Colombo, and she was back in the thick of missionary work again. She wrote another letter to her mother in which she said, "...the pain is over now and I am strong for the battle again."

That was Amy's opinion of her health, but it was not the opinion of the mission doctor who examined her. The doctor told Amy she had "brain exhaustion" and needed complete rest! Amy tried to rest the best she could, but she kept seeing so much mission work that needed to be done, enough work to last her a lifetime.

Amy stubbornly refused to even consider leaving Ceylon; that is, until November 27, 1894. That morning when Amy returned from a meeting she found a letter waiting for her. As she turned it over she recognized the return address, Broughton Grange, but not the handwriting. Who besides Robert Wilson would be writing to her from the Grange? She tore the envelope open. The letter was from Robert Wilson's son William. In the letter, William told Amy that his father had suffered a serious stroke and had asked her to come home immediately.

If Robert Wilson wanted Amy, nothing on earth would keep her away. Amy whirled into action, and within twenty-four hours she was on her way back to England. To get there faster, she booked passage only as far as Naples, Italy. From there she would travel across Europe by train, cross the English Channel by boat, and then go by train again on to London, where her mother would meet her. If all went well, she hoped to arrive in England by her twenty-seventh birthday. Her plan sounded good, but in truth, Amy was still seriously ill, and there were many days during the sea voyage from Ceylon when she didn't even leave her bunk. There were days when she didn't eat a thing and days when her ever-present diary was left completely blank.

Amy disembarked the ship in Naples, but she had little strength to get herself to the train station and onto the train for Rome. Not to mention changing trains in Rome for Paris or getting across town in Paris to board another train for Calais. And then there was crossing the English Channel. Just as she had been on her arrival in Japan, Amy was at the mercy of strangers. And strangers were kind to her. First Italian people and then French people saw she was in need of help. Kind strangers escorted her from one train to the next, until finally on December 15, 1894, Amy arrived in London.

Amy was met at the station by her mother. She was so exhausted from the journey that she stepped off the train and fell into her mother's arms. She had heard no news on the trip and so was eager to find out whether Robert Wilson was still alive. Her mother assured her he was very much alive and looking forward to seeing her. But before she could make the trip up to Broughton Grange, she had to rest and regain her strength. It was nine days later, on Christmas Eve, before she was strong enough to make the train journey north to the Grange.

Robert Wilson was beginning to recover from his stroke, and seeing Amy was the best medicine he could possibly have hoped for. The two of them spent hours in the library together. Amy told him all about her missionary adventures, and he convinced her to have her letters home from Japan published in a book. Amy had so many wonderful insights and such a good way with words that it would be a shame not to give English Christians the opportunity to view missions work through her eyes. For the next six months, besides taking care of Robert Wilson, Amy gathered her letters into the manuscript for a book. She drew many of the sketches in the book herself, and William Wilson drew the rest. How different things were from the early days at the Grange when the Wilson brothers didn't want Amy around.

Amy titled the book *From Sunrise Land.* The book was an instant success, and within a few months of publication, it went into its second printing. Once Amy had finished the book, she began to wonder what to do next. The doctor said that her health was still delicate, much too delicate to attempt another missionary journey. As she puzzled over what to do, the weeks turned into months, and life for Amy fell into almost the same routine it had been in before she left for Japan. On the outside it looked as if nothing had really changed. But on the inside, Amy was a different person. She had experienced the mission field firsthand. She had worked through her views on national dress and on following "harmless" local customs like keeping idols, and she had learned how to hear God's voice and follow it. But what was she supposed to do with all of this experience that was now locked inside her? She began to pray hard.

Shortly afterwards, Amy received a letter from a friend in Bangalore, in southern India. Her friend was a nurse and in charge of a hospital supported by the Church of England's Zenana Mission Society. She told Amy that the climate in the mountains where Bangalore was located was very pleasant and healthy, not too hot and not too cold, with none of the extremes the climate in China or Japan had. She asked Amy whether she would consider coming to work with her in Bangalore. Amy was willing to consider anything, but she felt it was a little like "cheating" to take the easy way out and go to a place with a mild climate. On the other hand, she was eager to get back to the mission field, and it seemed unlikely that any doctor would let her go back to a place that had a harsh climate. Amy settled in her mind that if the Zenana Mission Society would accept her as a missionary, knowing her physical condition and that she did not belong to the Church of England, she would go to Bangalore.

After a series of interviews with the mission society, in July 1895, Amy was accepted on the spot to work in southern India. Once again the Keswick Society agreed to sponsor and support her. Three months later, Amy was again waving good-bye to Robert Wilson. They had just spent his seventieth birthday together, and because he was getting older, she knew this time it was unlikely she'd ever see him again. What she didn't know was that she would never again set foot in the British Isles. She had bought a one-way ticket to India, believing that was where God had called her. Indeed, it was the last ocean voyage she ever made. She would never leave India.

Chapter 9

A Fish out of Water

Amy retraced the path of her earlier journey to Japan: east through the Mediterranean Sea, south through the Suez Canal and the Red Sea, and on into the Indian Ocean. During the voyage she often sat on deck in a slatted wooden deckchair and looked out to sea. Always she had the same thing on her mind: What would India really be like? Every English person thought he or she knew about India. After all, it had been under British control since the seventeenth century. First it had been under the control of the British East India Company, and then in 1858 it came under direct British rule, becoming the most populous colony in the British Empire. Queen Victoria was known also as the Empress of India, and the country itself was called the "jewel in the empire's crown." It was very fashionable for young Englishmen to spend time in India. With sixty thousand British soldiers stationed there to keep the peace, there was plenty of opportunity for a young Englishman to make a name and a fortune for himself.

Fine teas, exotic spices, and raw cotton from India were for sale everywhere in England. Book stores sold novels and collections of stories of discovery and adventure set in India. But in truth, England had influenced India far more than India had influenced England. In India, English was the language of business and government, which was a good thing because there were fifteen major languages spoken there, not to mention over eight hundred local dialects. English rule, or Raj, as it was called, also had brought roads, railways, industry, and education to India.

English people who lived in India were in a class of their own. They had the best of everything. They could afford to surround themselves with large numbers of servants, because they were cheap to hire. The men went on elephant hunts and played cricket and cribbage, while the women held dinner parties, embroidered pillows, and conducted readings from Shakespeare. The children were sent home to attend boarding school in England. But they usually returned for summer, when whole families would retreat to hill stations in the mountains to avoid the fierce summer heat. In short, the English in India were pampered, and that was just the way they liked it.

Beyond tea, spices, cotton, and pampered life-styles, Amy wondered what India was really going to be like. What would God have for her to do among the three hundred million people who lived there? While she didn't know for sure what lay ahead, she knew her first step involved working with the Zenana Mission Society.

Finally the ship reached Madras on India's southeastern coast. Madras was called the "Gateway to the South." Crowds of people surged around the end of the gangway as Amy disembarked. Men offered to carry her bags or hail a carriage for her as she looked around for Mr. Arden, the Church Missionary Society secretary, whom Robert Wilson had arranged to meet her. Sure enough, he was there waiting. He weaved his way through the crowd to Amy, who heaved a sigh of relief to see him. They shook hands and greeted each other. Her adventure in India was certainly getting off to a better start than her Japanese experience had.

While Mr. Arden loaded her trunk into the horse-drawn carriage, Amy looked around. It was difficult to take in everything at once. She had never seen so many colors before. Every sari, the traditional dress that Indian women wore, was different, and each one seemed to be more vibrant than the last. There were peacock blue, iridescent orange, and yellow as bright as the sun. Tall, dark men with twisted white or orange turbans on their heads were everywhere, as were little girls with jangly bangles the length of their arms. Amy loved it all.

Mr. Arden took her to his home, where she was to spend her first three weeks in India before heading inland to Bangalore, where the Zenana mission hospital was located. Amy had decided to stay the three weeks in Madras because she wanted to arrive in Bangalore rested and in the best possible health. While staying with the Ardens, she asked questions about India of anyone who had time to answer them. She was particularly interested in the history of Christianity in southern India because that was where her new home was to be. She learned that according to tradition, Thomas, one of Jesus' twelve disciples, was captured and sold as a slave to a merchant who took him to South India. There Thomas was sold again, this time to a king named Gundobar, who put Thomas to work overseeing the building of his new palace. During the building, Thomas had the opportunity to talk to the king about the gospel, and as a result, the king became a Christian and was baptized. Amy was thrilled to hear there was a group of Christians in southern India who called themselves "Thomas Christians" and traced the roots of their church right back to the time of St. Thomas and King Gundobar.

A week after Amy arrived, another missionary, Louisa Randall, came to talk to her. Louisa was an Englishwoman about Amy's age and had brought a letter with her regarding a problem she had encountered. Several months earlier she had met a young Muslim girl who wanted to become a Christian. But unlike Buddhists in Japan, who would tolerate a Christian in the family, Muslim families became violently angry if someone in the family became a Christian. The Muslim girl knew that if she became a convert she would either be banished from her home and family forever or be killed by her brothers. Finally, the girl decided she didn't have the courage to give up everything, including possibly her life, to become a Christian, and so she decided to stay a Muslim.

In a letter to her supporters, Louisa had written about the Muslim girl's struggle. As a result, one of her supporters had written back and complained that the story was too depressing and suggested that Louisa might brighten it up with a "happy ending." The response had upset Louisa, and she now wondered whether she'd done the right thing by telling the girl's story in the first place. She came to ask Amy her thoughts on the matter. Should she rewrite the girl's story, perhaps making the ending a little more vague and less depressing for her supporters? Amy was appalled. How could any Christian try to bully a missionary into inventing a happy ending when there was none? The truth is the truth, Amy told Louisa, and nothing, not even pressure from supporters, should cause a missionary to swerve from telling it.

Strangely enough, it wouldn't be long before Amy herself would be tested on this. She would find out that telling the truth was not always popular, even among Christians.

Finally, Amy's three weeks with the Ardens was up, and she began the two-hundred-thirty-mile trip from Madras to Bangalore. The trip had seemed so easy when she studied it on the globe in Robert Wilson's library. But that was back in England, and now as Amy sat on the train headed west toward Bangalore, she felt as though the trip would take forever. Villages and temples rolled past the train window where she sat, but she was having a hard time focusing on them. A servant brought her a cup of tea, but she didn't have enough strength to lift it to her lips. Amy realized she was sick again and getting sicker by the minute. This time she had dengue fever, or "breakbone fever," as it is also known. Indeed, Amy felt as though every bone in her body was broken. She could barely lift herself out of her seat when the conductor announced that the train was pulling into the station at Bangalore. She dragged herself off the train and into the arms of a waiting Zenana missionary. It was the exact opposite of the way she'd planned to make her entrance, but she was too ill to care. She was whisked off and admitted to the very hospital she'd come to serve in.

It took Amy several weeks to recover. As she lay in her hospital bed, waves of homesickness often swept over her. She would be homesick for her mother and Robert Wilson in England, homesick for Barclay Buxton, Misaki San, and the Christians in Hirose, Japan. Sometimes she was even homesick for the missionary work she never got to do in China! It seemed to Amy she would be better off almost anywhere than in the hospital, taking up the valuable time of missionaries whom she'd come to work alongside.

Slowly, as she started to feel stronger, Amy began to get involved in the daily routine of the Zenana Mission Society. One of the first things she did was attend a monthly staff social evening. It was at this gathering that the differences between Amy and many of the other missionaries began to show. The scene was innocent enough. The missionary women sat in a circle under the lamplight, quietly embroidering handkerchiefs with French knots and satin stitch. One of the men from the mission read an article on the partnership of missionaries and local Christians. The other men sat and listened and nodded occasionally. When the man had finished reading, a discussion was started. Mainly the men spoke, but occasionally a woman would look up from her embroidery and offer an opinion. As the discussion progressed, the question was raised as to who could name a single Indian Christian who would do Christian work without being paid by a missionary or the church to do it. The women continued poking their needles in and out of their fabric, while the men frowned and thought about the question. A minute past, then two and three. It seemed no one knew of anyone. "Oh, well," said one of the men with a nervous laugh. "One can't really blame them." At that moment, a servant brought in hot tea and cucumber sandwiches, and everyone's attention was soon diverted to the refreshments.

Amy laid down her embroidery. She sat in shock while the others drank tea and ate sandwiches. She wondered whether what she'd just heard could be true. In southern India, where tradition says St. Thomas brought the gospel message all the way from Israel, where Syrian Christians had a thriving community by the fourth century, and where hundreds of missionaries from many denominations had labored for centuries, could it be that not one Christian understood the joy of volunteering time to serve God? Surely it couldn't be? Amy thought of the shawlies in Belfast who had gone without sleep and had willingly given up their two precious days off a month to help with the work of The Welcome. Whenever she had needed someone to fill in at a service or to sweep the hall, the shawlies had been there, cheerfully, freely, gladly, willingly offering their time to do their part in reaching others with the gospel message. Of course, Amy didn't think it was always wrong to pay a person for his or her labor, but the thought that there was not one person who would work purely out of love for God left her speechless.

Amy looked at the other missionaries sitting and sipping tea from china cups. Shouldn't they all be on their knees begging God to forgive them for failing to inspire any devotion in the local population?

Instead, they passed around another plate of sandwiches, this time with watercress and tomato on them. Amy couldn't believe it.

This was not the only shock Amy had in her first few days with the mission. The more she saw of the missionary station, the more things bothered her. When she asked to visit the new-converts class, she was told there wasn't one; it wasn't needed. There hadn't been a new-converts class in years. Again, Amy could hardly believe what she was hearing. When she asked why there was no new-converts class, as part of the answer, one of the missionaries who'd served with the mission in Bangalore for many years explained the Hindu caste system to Amy.

All Hindus are divided into four castes, or groups. Every Hindu person is born into the same caste as his or her parents. Those in the top caste are called *Brahmans*, and they are religious and political leaders. Then there are the *Kshatriyas*, who are warriors; the *Vaisyas*, who are farmers and tradesmen; and the *Sudras*, who are laborers and servants. Below them are the lowest of the low, those who do not belong to a caste. They are called *untouchables*. When the caste system was first established, it was done as a way to organize society. It was much like the kings, lords, noblemen, and serfs of medieval England. But as the centuries passed, more and more rules were made about how different castes could relate to one another, and new castes within the main caste groups were formed. By the time

Amy arrived in Bangalore there were several thousand castes and many rules, some harsh, that were very strictly enforced. For example, a person could not eat food prepared by a member of a lower caste or marry out of his or her caste. Untouchables were left to do the work no one else would do. They had to clean up after cremation ceremonies, prepare animal hides, and rinse out chamber pots. Other Hindus would have nothing to do with them. Their caste forbade such contact. Untouchables could not drink water from the same well or even attend the same churches as people from higher castes for fear their shadow might touch someone of another caste and make them unclean. Amy nodded. She had seen the untouchables in Madras dressed in rags, their eyes staring at the ground.

The longtime missionary with the Zenana Mission Society went on to tell Amy about the hold Hinduism had over people. Loyalty was everything to a Hindu. The loyalty of a wife to her husband led to the practice of *suttee,* which the English were trying to wipe out. Suttee meant that when a man died it was the duty of his widow to commit suicide by throwing herself into the cremation fire with him. Sometimes the widow needed "a little help" to do this, but it was considered the right and loyal thing to do. The same was true of religion. A Hindu who converted to Christianity was labeled an infidel. To other Hindus, Christian converts had become disloyal to their religion, their society, and their family. As a result, they often were killed by members of their own family to prevent them from bringing any more disgrace to the family.

Amy thought back to Louisa's letter and its lack of a "happy ending." She was beginning to see the hold Hinduism had over every part of life in India. "But isn't the power of God greater than the power of Hinduism?"

"Yes, it should be," sighed the longtime missionary. "But in reality it does not seem to be so." And then he gave Amy a challenge: Would she pray and ask God why they were not seeing any Hindu converts? Of course she would. She started to pray about it right away. She had come to India to see God work in the lives of Indian people, and she, as much as anyone, wanted to know why it wasn't happening.

One of the things that Amy felt to be a barrier was that even though the mission society ran a school, most of the teachers were Hindus or Muslims. Again Amy spoke to the older missionary. She asked him what was the point of employing people from other religions to teach in the school. Wasn't the point of a Christian school to influence students toward Christianity? How could this happen if only a few of the teachers were Christians? The missionary told her it wasn't as easy as she might think to find Christians who would teach. Besides, weren't Hindu or Muslim teachers better than no teachers at all? Not to Amy they weren't! At least not in a Christian school. Amy told the missionary about the time she'd been short of workers at The Welcome and that many people had offered to help out of a sense of social concern. She had turned them all down, however, and waited for God to provide her with committed Christians who would serve others out of love for Him. Why couldn't the mission school apply the same principle? She knew it worked; she'd seen it work firsthand.

There were no easy answers, and although many of the missionaries liked Amy, her questions began to make some of them uncomfortable.

In her diary, Amy wrote, "I am beginning to feel like a fish out of water." Of course, fish do not last long out of water. Although Amy was trying hard to get along, trying hard to learn the Tamil language, and trying hard to fit into the British Empire missionary mold, it wasn't working. Something had to happen to get her back "in the water," and it had to happen soon.

Chapter 10

Going Native

A my dug her heels into the side of Laddie, the horse she was riding. Her long, dark brown hair streamed behind her as Laddie galloped along the pine-tree-lined trail. At first she hadn't wanted to leave Bangalore, but now that she was out of the city it felt good to be free. She was almost looking forward to the change of climate at Kotagiri, a hill-station retreat three thousand feet up in the Nilgiri Hills, where English people liked to go to relax and get away from the monsoon rains that fell during April and May.

As she galloped ahead, Amy looked back at the rest of the party she was traveling with. The group had just rounded a corner and come into sight. And what a sight they were! Her three fellow missionaries were being carried in sedan chairs—chairs with long poles on either side that were carried on the shoulders of eight servants. Behind the sedan chairs came Saral, carrying a light load of clothing, and then twelve other servants, all big, strong men, and all laboring under the burden of a box or a trunk, the missionaries' luggage. The servants were transporting everything from badminton rackets and nets to a matching set of folding chairs. Already, on the trip up to Kotagiri, Amy had passed one family with a piano being carried on a bullock cart, and another family with an iron bathtub among its vacation equipment.

Amy turned her attention back to the trail ahead. The procession behind her represented everything she didn't like about India. It took thirty-six servants to transport four English people and all of their "necessary" belongings from Bangalore up to the hill station of Kotagiri so the missionaries could have some rest. *Don't the servants need rest a hundred times more than we do?* Amy quizzed herself as she rode on. She longed to live life simply, free from morning and afternoon teas, handiwork circles, and cricket matches. She wanted to be free to reach out to Indian people. She wanted to get to know them as individuals and not just as servants. But how could she do this? She was an Englishwoman surrounded by Indian servants. The English weren't supposed to treat Indians as anything other than servants.

As she rode along smelling the wonderful oils from the pine trees and listening with delight to the sounds of a thousand birds, she came up with an idea. Why not move in with an Indian family? After all, she could learn the Tamil language far more easily and get to know Indians much better if she lived among them. As she turned the idea over and over in her mind she could see only one problem, but it was a big problem. "Going native," as identifying too closely with the local people was known in the missionary community, was greatly frowned upon. A person who went native was considered to be letting down the whole mission by giving up "civilized" English traditions. Such action was seen as nothing less than shunning Queen Victoria and the empire. Still Amy couldn't get the idea out of her mind. But how could she make it work? What she needed was someone who was well respected in the English missionary community who would support her in her plan. The trouble was, Amy didn't know anyone who thought living like a native was anything less than crazy.

Finally she arrived at Kotagiri, and straightaway she was in the middle of another problem. Problems seemed to follow Amy wherever she went. She just couldn't get used to being an empire lady. Her problem this time was that Kotagiri was a favored destination for the English, including missionaries, precisely because there were so few Indians there. The Indians who were there were mostly servants who knew their place and kept well out of sight whenever possible. Amy had brought Saral with her, but she treated her not as a servant but as a friend and assistant, just like she'd treated Misaki San in Japan. Amy expected to share her room with Saral during her stay in Kotagiri, but the very idea was outrageous to the other English folk. Gossip quickly spread around Kotagiri that there was a small Irish upstart in town. People wanted to know who she thought she was, upsetting the whole social order of Kotagiri so she could have an Indian friend stay with her.

Finally, Amy gave in, and Saral stayed with the other servants. But the experience greatly disturbed Amy. It was not easy for her to see barriers between Christians. Yet her disappointment sparked in her the desire to someday find a way to break down such barriers.

While in Kotagiri, Amy continued to spend her six hours a day studying the Tamil language, just as she'd done in Bangalore. When she wasn't studying, she would explore the surrounding hills with Saral. But as they explored, Amy began to find that walking long distances made her very tired. Her body was letting her down again. Since coming to India, her health had deteriorated, and most of her coworkers told her they didn't think she'd last a year in India. Despite her weakened body, Amy was determined to build up her strength and prove them all wrong.

After several days in Kotagiri, Amy and Saral traveled on to another hill station called Oota-camund. The English called the place "Ooty." (Some people who couldn't afford to stay there called it

"Snooty Ooty.") Amy couldn't wait to get to Ooty, not because she needed any more pampering by servants, but because there was going to be some Keswick-style meetings held there. One of the scheduled speakers was Thomas Walker, chairman of the Church Missionary Society in India, the society that oversaw the work of the Zenana Mission with whom Amy worked in Bangalore. Amy looked forward to hearing him speak. Everyone seemed to have something good to say about Thomas Walker. Actually, everyone referred to him as Iyer Walker, *Iyer* being an Indian term of respect. Iyer Walker was a veteran missionary and could speak the Tamil language better than most native Indians. He also knew more about the history of southern India than any other English person.

From all she'd heard about him, Amy thought she had a pretty good idea of what to expect as she made her way to the meeting where Iyer Walker was to speak. She imagined him to be elderly, perhaps a slightly younger version of Robert Wilson. Amy tucked her Tamil grammar book under her arm, just in case Iyer Walker turned out to be a boring speaker. That way, she could pass the time more usefully by studying her grammar.

Amy never opened the grammar book during the service, but her eyes were certainly opened. Iyer Walker was nothing like she'd imagined. He was a young man, about thirty-six years of age, only seven years older than Amy. He had jet black hair with not a hint of gray, and when he spoke, there was only one word to describe his speech—a very modern word—*electrifying*. Amy listened to everything he said, wondering how a man so young could be so wise. As she listened, in one corner of her mind, Amy had another thought. Maybe, just maybe, Iyer Walker was the person to convince to support her plan to live with an Indian family. Everything Amy wanted to do in India seemed to fit in with what Iyer Walker was saying in his address.

At the close of the meeting, Amy rushed forward to introduce herself to Iyer Walker. From his raised eyebrows, Amy could tell he'd already heard about her. It was hot and stuffy in the tent where the meeting was being held, and so Iyer Walker and his wife invited Amy to take a stroll with them in a nearby rose garden. After discussing the sermon topic for about ten minutes, Amy got up the courage to ask Iyer Walker her question. "Mr. Walker," she began, her eyes looking down at the ground. "I'm trying to learn the Tamil language as quickly as I can, but I'm frustrated. I would like to learn faster. I think I could learn more if I lived in a mud hut with a Tamil family and talked to them all day in Tamil instead of English." She looked up. Iyer Walker didn't say anything. "What do you think?" she pressed him.

"You wouldn't survive there for very long," he said bluntly.

"I'd rather burn out in a Tamil house than rust out on a mission compound," Amy replied defensively.

"That's just what might happen to you," Iyer

Walker said without a trace of humor in his voice or on his face.

Amy couldn't believe it. She'd thought Iyer Walker would agree with her. But instead he'd made rude comments about her plan. She decided she didn't like him one bit. He had too many opinions! Things were not going at all as she had planned. Maybe, somewhere deep inside, Amy realized she'd met her match. Iyer Walker was just as stubborn and opinionated as she was. And they had one thing more in common, though neither of them knew it at the time. They were both about to make major decisions that would link them together in ministry for the rest of their lives.

Iyer Walker had been chairman of the Church Missionary Society in India since 1885, but he'd finally had enough. The job seemed to offer only endless paperwork and the occasional chance to speak at a conference. He knew the frustration Amy was feeling, though he didn't tell her so at the time, perhaps because he was a senior missionary who wasn't supposed to feel that way. Like Amy, he had come to India to live among the people, not to work in a stuffy office all day seeing mostly white faces. He was ready for a change.

By the end of the week, when the meetings in Ooty were over, Amy had softened some in her view of Iyer Walker. It was a good thing she had, because Iyer Walker made her an interesting offer. He could see Amy was not doing well with all the restrictions of a traditional missionary setting, so he asked her if she would like to come and live with

him and his wife and learn the Tamil language from
them. He would arrange everything with the
Zenana Mission Society if she said yes. The longer
Amy was away from Bangalore, the less she wanted
to go back, so she agreed to move in with the
Walkers. The day Amy moved into the Walkers'
home, Iyer Walker himself was moving out of his
mission office. He had resigned as chairman. So the
Walkers and Amy Carmichael both began new
chapters of their lives on the same day.

Iyer Walker had long dreamed of having a band
of evangelists who would travel throughout the
Tirunelveli district of southern India. The Tirunelveli
district was located in the center of the southern tip
of India, about an equal distance inland from the
Gulf of Mannar to the east and the Arabian Sea to
the west. It was separated from the Arabian Sea by
a range of high mountains called the Western Ghats.
Iyer Walker had decided it was time to make his
dream there a reality, so along with Amy, the
Walkers moved into a small town in the district,
called Pannaivilai.

By the end of July 1897, when they were finally
settled into the simple bungalow that was their new
home, Amy was well on her way to mastering the
difficult Tamil language. The Walkers had proved to
be good teachers.

During her first year living with the Walkers,
Amy had come to realize that Iyer Walker was
indeed just as stubborn as she was. The two of them
came to an arrangement that allowed them to work

together and tell each other what they were thinking without hurting the other's feelings. This was a
good thing, because they both had plenty to say to
each other. Also during her first year in Pannaivilai,
something happened that Amy would remember as
a warning for the rest of her life. It involved a fif-
teen-year-old girl named Pappamal.

Pappamal lived in a nearby town called
Palamcottah, the center for Christian activity in the
region. Pappamal had heard the gospel message
and had told Amy she wanted to become a
Christian. Of course, this meant having to make a
very difficult decision for everyone concerned. If
Pappamal became a Christian, she would have to be
smuggled away from her family because there was
no doubt they would try to have her killed. It also
would mean considerable hardship for the missior-
aries. With each conversion of a high-caste person, a
wave of nasty persecution followed. The entire
Hindu community would leave no stone unturned
to make life difficult for the Christians. The people
would force mission schools to close, vandalize
churches, beat up missionaries, and file endless law-
suits. By helping Pappamal, the missionaries would
be hurting themselves. Still, after the Christians at
Palamcottah had weighed the situation, they
decided that if Pappamal had the faith to "defect"
from Hinduism, they would do whatever it took to
keep her safe, regardless of the consequences.

It was decided that Amy would smuggle
Pappamal away to Ooty, where an Indian woman

who was a Christian would look after her. It was a dangerous journey as they tried to avoid people along the way. Thankfully, they both made it safely, and Amy was thrilled to have played a part in rescuing a girl from Hinduism. She decided such acts were what missionary life in India was about.

Meanwhile in Palamcottah, trouble was brewing. Once word got around that Pappamal had left her family and broken caste, hardly anyone would speak to the missionaries. Indian parents pulled their children out of school, while other Indians declared they would rather die than visit the medical clinic run by the missionaries.

Farther north in the mountains at Ooty, the Bible woman, as most Indian Christian women were normally called, was faithfully watching over Pappamal, watching a little too closely for Pappamal's liking, as it turned out. One night the Bible woman was sure she had seen a man loitering around Pappamal's window. The next morning she quizzed her, and a very different story from the one Pappamal had told the missionaries came tumbling out. No, she wasn't a Christian, and she didn't want to become one. What she wanted was to be married to a man from another caste. Of course, her parents would never allow it, so she and her boyfriend had come up with a plan. Pappamal would say she'd become a Christian and would escape from her house to be with the missionaries. The couple had hoped the missionaries would then smuggle her out of the area. So far their plan had worked perfectly.

Once Pappamal was out of the area, her boyfriend would declare himself to be a Christian also, and then they would get married. But that part of their plan was not going to work, not if the Bible woman had anything to say about it! She was furious that Pappamal and her boyfriend had, for selfish reasons, endangered the lives and the work of missionaries in and around Palamcottah. She sent a message to Pappamal's father right away, telling him he could come and get his Hindu daughter. Pappamal's father sent a return message saying he didn't want to see his daughter anymore. But the Bible woman would not give up. She marched Pappamal all the way back to Palamcottah herself and left her sitting on her father's doorstep.

Returning Pappamal didn't end matters, however. Pappamal's parents filed a lawsuit against the missionaries, claiming, because Pappamal was under sixteen years of age, that they had "seduced" a minor. Pappamal herself filed another lawsuit against the missionaries, claiming she had been kidnapped by them and held against her will. The whole mess took more than a year and a lot of time in court to straighten out. Some Hindus never forgave the missionaries for their "seduction" and "kidnapping" and kept their children well out of reach of the Christians.

Amy watched as the whole situation unfolded. She was amazed at how easily she and many others had been taken in by a trick. *How did it happen?* She asked herself over and over. As she thought about it, something inside her told her it wouldn't be the last trick that would be played on her. She decided that in the future, she had better keep her eyes open and her wits about her.

Chapter 11

The Starry Cluster

Amy was discouraged. She finally realized that Saral, her friend and helper for more than a year, would not be back. Saral had gone with Amy when she moved from Bangalore to live with the Walkers. She was a wonderful Christian, and together they had been the beginnings of a team of women Amy wanted to form to share the gospel message in the surrounding towns and villages. But that was before Saral had told Amy she needed to visit her aging mother. After a month away, she'd sent word she would be another week, and then another week, and another week after that. Finally, when yet another week passed, Amy knew that Saral wouldn't be coming back. Now she was faced with finding a replacement. But where was she going to find another woman who was free enough and willing enough to travel with her throughout the countryside sharing the gospel?

In India, most girls were married off by the time they were sixteen years old. Many girls were married much younger than that. No Indian husband would give his wife permission to travel around sharing the gospel message. Most Hindu and Muslim men in India would not even give their wives permission to leave the house, much less their village. Men had total control over their wives. So where was Amy going to find a group of mature women who had the courage to defy custom and travel with her? She wondered if such women even existed. Still, she committed herself to pray about it. She wrote to her friends in England and Ireland, asking them to pray about it as well.

Around this time, Amy finished her basic Tamil language training with Iyer Walker. She was eager to get out and about around Pannaivilai and use her new language skills meeting and talking to people. She remembered how wearing a kimono in Japan had helped her blend in with the people and put them at ease as they talked, so she decided to start wearing a sari as she went about Pannaivilai. Saris were the customary dress of Indian women. However, there was one big difference between Japan and India. India was a British colony, Japan was not. English people in India were supposed to show in all they did that English culture was better than Indian culture. This meant not only being careful to hold a teacup with the little finger sticking out but also wearing clothes that would be fashionable in the motherland, as England was known. If an English person decided to do something the Indian way, that was seen as letting the team down. Amy decided to do something the Indian way, and she soon faced a barrage of criticism from other English people. The only person who offered her any support was Iyer Walker. He could see the advantages for Amy in wearing a sari. No one else could. As Amy began to wear her sari, she became the subject of a lot of gossip and criticism, even from other Christians.

Saris came in every color of the rainbow. Rich women often owned a hundred or more of them, each one made of richly embroidered silk. A poor woman, on the other hand, would have only two or three saris made of plain cotton fabric. The poorest women usually owned only a single white sari. As much as she loved the bright colors and embroidered silk, Amy chose a simple sari made of plain white cotton. As she wrapped herself in the twenty-foot strip of cotton fabric for the first time, she prayed her sari would open doors for her to speak to Hindu women.

There was one woman to whom Amy felt particularly drawn. Her name was Ponnammal, and she was a very attractive, twenty-three-year-old widow. Her father-in-law was a deacon in the local church, but like so many Indian Christians at that time, he still followed many Hindu traditions, such as keeping idols and not breaking caste. But his worst Hindu practice, in Amy's opinion, was the way he treated Ponnammal. When an Indian woman married, she became the property of her husband, and if he died, she didn't return to her parents but instead became the property of her father-in-law. Ponnammal's father-in-law made good use of Ponnammal around the house. She was basically his servant, doing the cleaning, cooking the meals, and carrying the water. She was never allowed to visit her friends or relatives, but she could go to church on Sundays. It was at church that Ponnammal and Mrs. Walker became friends. Mrs. Walker could see that Ponnammal had a lot of abilities that were going unused, so she had her husband put pressure on Ponnammal's father-in-law to allow her to teach Sunday school.

Ponnammal loved being involved with the Sunday school. She was a born teacher with a strong faith in God. Amy was thrilled to see an Indian woman holding a responsible position in the church, and she began to wonder whether there was any way she and Ponnammal might be able to work more closely together. She mentioned this possibility to Ponnammal, who told Amy she would love to become more involved, but there was no way her father-in-law would agree to it.

Amy talked to the church pastor and Iyer Walker about her working with Ponnammal, and after much persuasion from both men, Ponnammal's father-in-law felt shamed into letting Ponnammal go. He quickly changed his mind, though, but it was too late! As soon as Ponnammal heard that her father-in-law had given his permission for her to work with Amy, she ran to her and would not go back. Her father-in-law became very angry with Amy. He called her a *"musal* missie." Musal is the Tamil word for hare, and Ponnammal's father-in-law called Amy a hare because she had been so fast in moving Ponnammal out of the house. But like it or not, he had given his permission in front of witnesses for Ponnammal to leave, and he had no legal way to get her back. Still, Amy was a little nervous. She knew she'd gained a wonderful helper in Ponnammal, but she had also gained an enemy in her father-in-law. She didn't know how or when, but she was certain he would strike back at her and try to take Ponnammal away.

Not long after Ponnammal came to work with Amy, another Indian woman joined the band. Her name was Sellamutthu, and her family was glad to get rid of her. Sellamutthu was useless to them for one simple reason: she had only one arm. She'd lost her right arm in an accident when she was a small child, and now she was worth nothing to her family. A woman with only one arm could never find a husband. Who would want a wife who could not pound corn, spin cotton, or even hold a baby properly? So Sellamutthu's family had hidden her out of sight in a filthy room at the back of the house. Somehow, Sellamutthu heard about Amy and the band of Christians she hoped to form and asked to be released to join them. Her family willingly let her go, though they were sure it would not be long before she came crawling back. After all, what use would a one-armed worker be to an English-woman? To Sellamutthu's parents' surprise, Amy gladly welcomed her. She would use any woman God sent her way. It mattered not one bit that she had only one arm.

Soon after, another woman talked to Amy about joining her group. The woman's name was Marial, and she told Amy that God had called her to share the gospel message. There was just one problem: She was married. At first Amy didn't want married women in her group; it would be too difficult. But Amy agreed to meet with Marial's husband, and she was pleasantly surprised when she met him. Although he did not want to preach, he acknowl-edged that Marial did, and he wanted her to have the opportunity to do so. This was a very unusual attitude for an Indian man to have, and Amy thought it might be another trick of some kind. But as she prayed about it, she felt a peace in her heart. So she invited Marial to join the team. Marial's hus-band came along as the group's cook!

Finally, Amy had gathered a small team of Indian women who wanted to step out of their cul-tural roles to share the gospel message. The next question was what to call the group. Amy asked the other women, who decided on the name "Starry Cluster." Amy laughed. It wasn't quite the name she would have chosen, but it would do fine. Besides,

the Bible said that those who lead people to righteousness will shine like stars (Daniel 12:3). Amy
and the Starry Cluster prayed that their work would
indeed turn people to righteousness throughout the
Tirunelveli district with its four thousand Hindu
temples.

Around Christmas 1897, the Starry Cluster
began their work among the surrounding villages.
They traveled on a bandy, a springless cart pulled
by two bullocks. The bandy had a curved, woven
grass mat for a roof, but no sides. It was even more
bone jarring to ride on than a rickshaw. It was also a
very exhausting way to travel, especially during the
heat of the day. It would have been much more
comfortable to travel during the cool of the evening,
but they dared not do that. Indian women, even
those dressed in plain saris, tended to wear a lot of
jewelry. They wore nose rings, toe rings, earrings,
bracelets, and anklets, all made from gold. The jewelry was a sign of their family's wealth and standing in the community. No Tamil woman would
think of going out without wearing all of her jewelry. Of course, this made a woman a good target
for robbers. When it came to jewelry, the women in
Amy's group were no different from other Tamil
women. Traveling at night they would have been an
easy target for an ambush and robbery. There were
always thieves on the roads between the villages
waiting to ambush some unsuspecting person.

Most of the towns and villages in the region
were surrounded by city walls. After the bone-jarring

trip in the bandy, the Starry Cluster would search out a campsite just outside the wall to pitch their tents. A shaded spot by a stream was always their first choice. From there they approached each village in more or less the same manner. Just after dawn they would walk together through the city gates and go to the marketplace. In the market they would break into pairs and sit in a quiet place, usually under a tree or on the edge of a veranda. It was then a matter of waiting and praying. Often a woman or a small group of women would search them out and ask them questions. At midday, the Starry Cluster returned to camp for lunch and a Bible study. Following the Bible study, they spent time praying for the people they'd talked to in the morning. Then it was back to the village for the rest of the afternoon. The women would hold an open-air meeting and sing and preach in the streets. They used a tiny organ they carried with them to accompany the singing. As expected, only women and children stopped to listen to them. The men were not one bit interested in anything an ignorant woman had to say!

It was hot, hard work, but the women didn't complain. They were all glad to be doing something useful for God. Amy especially liked those times when Iyer Walker joined them. He had started a similar group for men, and sometimes the two groups would get together and travel to a village in convoy.

The Starry Cluster never knew what to expect when they entered a village. One time Amy was involved in a deep discussion with a woman of high caste. During their conversation, Amy reached out and touched the woman's arm. The woman began screaming hysterically. Amy instantly realized what she had done. It was not acceptable for a person of lesser or no caste to touch someone of a higher caste. It was no use apologizing; it would do no good. The opportunity to share the gospel message with the woman had been lost.

Another time, a widow named Blessing traveled with the Starry Cluster. Blessing was a new convert whom Amy was teaching about the Christian faith. Amy and Blessing met a woman who stopped to talk with them. As the woman chatted away, Amy was impressed with her knowledge of classical literature. It was clear the woman had a good education, something that was very rare among Indian women at that time. Being a Christian, Blessing felt free to join in the conversation, though from her speech it was easy to tell she was from a lower caste. Under the caste system, she would not have dared talk to this woman. Unfortunately, the woman was very insulted that a peasant woman from a lower caste had spoken to her. She began to insult Blessing, who stood smiling. When the woman finished her ranting, Blessing looked her right in the eyes and said, "I'm a new Christian. I am only one month old in my faith, and what you say is true. I do not know much. But in my heart I have God's peace and joy. And isn't joy better than all the learning in the world?"

The woman gathered her sari around her, gave Amy a withering look, and stormed off. After she had gone, Amy asked Blessing why the woman had such a good education. Blessing's answer would affect Amy the rest of her life. She told Amy the woman was a temple prostitute who would have been given to the Hindu priests when she was very young. The priests would have educated her in exchange for her services throughout the years. Furthermore, Blessing didn't know of a single temple prostitute who had ever become a Christian. In fact, only the older ones, like the woman they had just talked to, were allowed outside the temple. The younger girls and teenagers were kept as virtual prisoners until they could remember no other life except that of being a temple prostitute.

Amy was discouraged by what she heard from Blessing, but fortunately there were other things to encourage her along the way, such as the Starry Cluster. The women were turning into real missionaries. It was normal to give workers, even Christian workers, a daily allowance, or *batta*, as it was called. When they all returned home from their first mission journey, Amy paid the women their *batta*. An hour later they all filed back into the dining room, where Amy sat writing a letter. One by one they placed their *batta* on the table. Ponnammal spoke up. "We don't need this money. We can do without it. We would rather you spent it on missionary work."

Tears came to Amy's eyes. She thought of the staff get-together back in Bangalore where not one missionary had been able to name a single Indian Christian who would work without pay. But God had given Amy a whole Starry Cluster full of women willing to work for nothing because of their devotion to God.

Another encouraging thing occurred several weeks later. Marial's husband, the group's cook, was walking along beside the bandy as the group made their way home after spending several days in a village to the south. He usually didn't say much, so it was hard to know what he was thinking. But as the group rolled across some rice fields, he turned to Marial riding in the bandy and said, "It's time to take off your jewelry. Wearing jewelry is not suitable for the life of following Jesus we are living." Right there in the bandy, Marial stripped off her nose ring, bangles, and toe rings and handed them to her husband. She showed no hint of emotion at getting rid of her jewelry.

Ponnammal and Sellamutthu watched wide-eyed. How could Marial take off her jewelry like that? People would think she was one of the lowest of the low, an untouchable. What a huge insult it would be to her husband's family, and yet it was her husband who had asked her to take it off. The rest of the way home, Ponnammal and Sellamutthu remained silent. When they got back to Pannaivilai, they spoke to Amy. "Marial has taken off her jewelry," Ponnammal said. Amy nodded; she had seen her do it. "We are going to take off our jewelry, too," continued Ponnammal. "If I had loved Jesus more, I would have loved my jewels less." With that she bent down and began undoing her foot bangles. Sellamutthu followed her, and soon both of them were standing in front of Amy wearing no jewelry at all. Amy smiled at them both. It had taken a lot of courage to go against generations of custom, yet the women were prepared to do it because of their love for God.

Of course, not all Christians saw it that way. When Ponnammal's father-in-law heard what she had done, he was outraged. How could she take off her jewelry and look like a nobody! He stirred up as much anger and hatred in the church as he possibly could. He saw it as an opportunity to get rid of the Starry Cluster and get his daughter-in-law back. But as hard as he tried to stir up trouble, the pastor of the church would not speak out against Amy or the Starry Cluster. Instead, he told Amy that for the first time, many in his congregation were finally beginning to understand what it meant to be a Christian and follow Jesus.

Chapter 12

Let Me Stay in the Light

There was a village near Pannaivilai called Great Lake. The village had a Christian mission school where local boys, and even a few girls, were educated. Not one of the parents or children attending the school was a Christian, which had been true for the past sixty years. The villagers knew that the school was run by Christians, but they didn't worry in the slightest about their children's being influenced by Christianity. Even the youngest child knew better than to break caste. That was, until 1895, the same year Amy arrived in India. One of the girls in the school, who was thirteen years old at the time, was given a Bible by the school principal's wife. She read the Bible and became a secret Christian. Very secret. She didn't tell a single person about it, and she continued with all the family's Hindu practices. She went so far as to allow her brother to smear Siva's ashes on her forehead every morning. These ashes were worn by devout Hindus to show others their devotion to Hindu gods.

Three years later, the girl had finished school and was being kept at home, which was normal in Indian culture. In fact, she hadn't been outside the house once in two years. But as she spent many hours by herself doing household chores, she thought about what she had read in the Bible. Slowly she began to realize she didn't want to be a secret Christian anymore. Instead, she wanted to become an open believer. She wanted to pray with other Christians and go to Bible studies and share her faith with her family. She was also aware that confessing her belief in Christianity could cost her her life. Yet despite that possibility, she could no longer stand to live her faith in secret. She had heard her father and brother talking about the Starry Cluster, and even though they talked about the group in insulting terms, she felt strangely attracted to it.

One night, after everyone was asleep, the girl woke up. Shivers ran up and down her spine. Somehow she knew she had to escape. She had to get to the Starry Cluster. But what if someone saw her? She would be brought home in disgrace and beaten for sure, maybe even found dead at the bottom of a well shaft in the morning. But her desire to escape was too strong to worry about any potential consequences.

Slowly and carefully she stepped over her sleeping mother and tiptoed to the door. She turned the lock and pulled the door open. For the first time in two years, she smelled the fresh air of the garden. Keeping in the shadows with her ear attuned to every sound, she crept out of the village, along the rutted path, and over the bridge into Pannaivilai. Once there, she had no idea where to go next. She sneaked around Pannaivilai until she came to a large two-story house with a veranda around it. A banner over the front door told her she had come to the home of Christians. Suddenly, instead of being as quiet as possible, she had to make noise, and lots of it. She banged on the door and yelled, "Refuge! Refuge!" A sleepy Amy opened the door and let her in.

By the next morning, the village of Great Lake was in an uproar. The girl's father had discovered that his daughter was missing. That was bad enough, but to find she had run to Christians for refuge was too much to bear. It was an insult to the entire goldsmithing caste to which her family belonged. Her father would rather see her dead than have her break caste and stay with Christians. He mounted a campaign to get her back. But the girl, whom Amy named Jewel of Victory, stood her ground. She went to the village constable and gave a sworn statement to say she was sixteen years of age and was living with the Starry Cluster of her own free choice. Once that was done, there was nothing her father could do—legally, that is.

Unfortunately, there were a lot of other things he and the other men of the village could and did do. First, they burned down the school. This meant that none of the other children in the village would receive an education, but her father didn't seem to care. It was more important that the terrible thing his daughter had done would never happen again. Next they burned down the school principal's house and drove the school workers out of Great Lake village.

Jewel of Victory was safe with the Starry Cluster, but many people paid the price for her conversion. And the Starry Cluster would not be welcome again in Great Lake village. That was for certain! Indeed, until the turmoil died down, the women of the Starry Cluster decided they should work in the villages to the north of Pannaivilai. But they ran headlong into another crisis there. They were preaching in the streets of a village called Uncrowned King when an eleven-year-old girl named Arulai came by. Arulai was fetching water for her family at the same time the women were holding their meeting, and she stopped to listen to what the women had to say. Arulai had a bad temper, which she'd tried to control without much success. As she listened to the Starry Cluster, she watched Amy very closely. There was something about the Englishwoman in the simple, white cotton sari that fascinated her. When the meeting closed, Arulai overheard one of the women in the Starry Cluster say, "I was a lion, and God turned me into a lamb."

As she carried the water jar home, Arulai thought about what she'd overheard. A lion turned into a lamb, she said over and over to herself. There was nothing more wild and out of control than a lion or anything more gentle and sweet than a lamb. If God could turn a lion into a lamb, then maybe, just maybe, He could also control her temper. As the days went by, Arulai became more and more sure that He could. Finally one day, she announced to her parents that she wanted to go and live with the Englishwoman in the white cotton sari. Her family was convinced that Amy had sprinkled some magic powder on their daughter to make her want to leave home. Amy was quickly earning a new name in the area—"child-snatching Amma." (*Amma* is the Tamil word for mother.)

Arulai kept talking about going to live with Amy until her whole family were so sick of listening to her they sent her off for a long visit at her uncle's house. That was a big mistake. Arulai's family didn't realize that her uncle lived in the next village to Pannaivilai, and it was only a short walk for Arulai to slip away and visit Amy. And that is what she did. She made so many visits that in the end, her uncle said she could stay for Bible studies as well. As Arulai learned more and more about the Christian God, she became convinced He was the true God, and she became a convert. She began to speak out boldly about her growing faith. Of course, this really upset her family, and they soon whisked her away from her uncle's house.

Months passed, and Amy heard no news of her new friend. She prayed for her every day and hoped she would somehow be able to find a way to come back one day. Meanwhile, more trouble followed the Starry Cluster.

Children, it seemed, were the most drawn to Amy and her message. Unfortunately, horrible things sometimes happened to children whose parents thought they had been listening for too long to the bewitching child stealer. One girl was drugged by her family when she started to question Hindu ways. Her brain was affected by the drug, and she was never the same again. Other children were beaten or whipped or had hot peppers ground into their eyes. Arul Dasan, who turned out to be Arulai's cousin, was kept tied to a pillar in his house for days on end in the hope he would lose interest in Christianity. Every time Amy heard one of these stories, she thought of Arulai and prayed harder that God would bring her back to visit.

Finally in November, eight months after she'd last been seen by anyone in the Starry Cluster, Arulai appeared again. She arrived on the doorstep one morning, and Amy rushed out to greet her. It was a wonderful reunion, except for one thing. Arulai was sick and getting sicker by the minute. Amy helped her inside and laid her on the couch. Arulai did not know what was wrong with her; she just knew that she felt very weak and had an incredible headache. Finally, Amy put Arulai into her bed and stayed by her side day and night.

Sometimes she prayed for a miracle because she was sure a miracle was the only thing that could save Arulai's life.

As Arulai lay in Amy's bed close to death, a strange thing happened. Her father came to take her home, but when he saw how sick she was, he realized she could not be moved. Instead, he kept coming back regularly to see whether his daughter was well enough to take home. On those trips, he began to see how Amy cared for his daughter. He hated to admit it, but his daughter was getting more love and care with Amy and the Starry Cluster than she would get in her own home. Ever so slowly, his resolve to force Arulai to come home as soon as possible began to crumble. And ever so slowly, Arulai began to gather strength. Sometimes Amy would overhear her desperate prayers. "Please don't make me go back to the darkness, God. I am living in the light here. Let me stay in the light."

By the time Arulai was completely well again, her father had given up the demand that his now twelve-year-old daughter come home, and Arulai was allowed to stay on with the group in Pannaivilai.

Amy was always doing two or three things at once, and while she was nursing Arulai she was also writing a manuscript. Five years after she had sailed for India, the Keswick Convention still supported her. Fueled by the interest generated by *From Sunrise Land*, her book of letters from Japan, the Keswick Convention had asked Amy to write a book about India. It took many months of writing and rewriting, but finally Amy felt happy with the result. Then the question came, what to title the manuscript? Amy didn't want anything too grand or too flowery. She wanted something that was simple and to the point. Finally, she settled on the title *Things As They Are*. That said it all for Amy. It wasn't about things as she might want them to be in India, or things the way people in England imagined they might be. No, it was about things as they are.

Amy sent the manuscript off to the Keswick committee in England. She got it back from them much sooner than she'd expected. Inside with the manuscript was a note thanking her for all her hard work but suggesting she make a few changes. It seemed they felt her manuscript was a bit depressing to read. Perhaps, the editor suggested, it needed a lighter touch, more happy stories, and fewer stories about young children and women in unreachable situations. Again Amy was confronted with the desire of Christians in England for "happy missionary, happy ending" stories. She shook her head. If only the committee could have spent a few days with her, they would have quickly seen that for every Arulai, there were a thousand girls who were temple prostitutes or household slaves. Their lives did not have happy endings, and Amy would not pretend they did. She stuffed the manuscript in the bottom drawer of her desk.

Other mail came from England, and it was upsetting, too. Robert Wilson's sons wrote letter after letter begging Amy to come home to Broughton Grange. Their father asked for her every day; their father was getting weaker; their father had had another stroke. But Amy couldn't go back to England, especially now that she had Arulai to look after. Besides, she knew that God had called her to India, and she would not leave unless she was certain He was calling her elsewhere. Still, Amy did get homesick. She longed for someone from England to come and visit her. She wanted to show them the way things were and get a firsthand account of the state of Robert Wilson's health.

Her longing was rewarded toward the end of 1900. Two of her close friends from Manchester, Ella Crossley and Mary Hatch, announced that they had bought tickets and were on their way to see her. Amy was so glad to see them again. Of course, the first questions she wanted answered were, Had they seen Robert Wilson before they left, and How was he doing? Ella and Mary had visited him right before they left, and better yet, they had a letter for Amy that Robert Wilson had dictated to Ella. Amy ripped the envelope open and read what he had to say. One sentence particularly caught her attention: "I hope you will not let my sickness change any of your plans." Amy was grateful for his reassurance that she was doing the right thing staying in India.

Ella and Mary wanted to experience everything Amy had described to them in her letters. They were eager to climb aboard the bandy and travel the countryside with the Starry Cluster. Amy told them the story of Jewel of Victory and Arulai, who were now both a part of the cluster. The two women got to see a a side of India few Englishwomen ever saw.

One day the three of them entered a home where a child lay crying in a hammock. Amy picked up the child and held him tightly. She guessed he was about three years old. He continuously rubbed his eyes, which were red and nearly swollen shut. "How long has he been like this?" Amy asked his mother.

"About three months," the mother replied, "but he does not cry as loudly as he used to."

"What does the doctor say?" Amy asked in Tamil, while interpreting the conversation into English for Ella and Mary.

The mother looked down. "We will not take him to the doctor," she said hesitantly, and then added, "it would be breaking caste."

Amy hugged the little boy closer. Surely there could be an exception. The child was well on his way to blindness, if not death. How could it be against caste to get him medical help? She begged and pleaded with the mother to let her take the child to the nearest hospital. But the mother would not budge. Nothing mattered more to her than keeping caste, not even the possible death of her own little boy. Keeping caste was more important than keeping his life.

Ella and Mary emerged from the hut into the bright sunlight with tears streaming down their cheeks. Although they had been reading Amy's letters for years, the reality of experiencing firsthand what she had described was almost more than they could bear.

They asked Amy why she didn't write a book about conditions in India so that Christians in England and other places could pray for her and her workers. Amy shrugged her shoulders. Over the next several weeks, they asked the same question again and again. Finally, Amy opened the bottom drawer of her desk and took out the manuscript for *Things As They Are*. She handed it to Ella and Mary, who took turns reading it aloud to each other. When they finished, they were sure it had to be published. Christians needed to know the truth about India, the so-called jewel in the empire's crown.

Amy then showed them the letter from the Keswick committee about the manuscript. Ella and Mary shook their heads in disbelief. If only the committee could see what they had seen, then they would understand. *Things As They Are* was indeed a true picture of life in India and Amy's work there. Eventually the two women persuaded Amy to give them the manuscript to take back to England. They must have been two forceful women, because soon after their return to England, *Things As They Are* was published, complete with photos Ella had taken during her visit.

Meanwhile, back in India, Amy and the Starry Cluster were busier than ever going from village to village sharing the gospel message.

Chapter 13

Child-Stealing Amma

Iyer Walker, Amy, and the Starry Cluster had been working in and around the village of Dohnavur for nearly a year. They had intended to spend only three months in the area while Iyer Walker taught a small group of Bible students, but the three months had been stretched and stretched. And there was plenty to do. Dohnavur was a ramshackle little village that lay in the center of a densely populated area. From the village, the Starry Cluster fanned out through the countryside sharing the gospel message and meeting the usual mixed reactions from people. But after a year away, it was time for them all to head back home to Pannaivilai.

The trip back to Pannaivilai took them right past the village of Great Lake, from which Jewel of

Victory had escaped. In the very early morning of March 6, 1902, long, long before the sun was due to rise, they were on the final leg of their journey home. (They were able to travel at night now because word had got around that the women of the Starry Cluster wore no jewelry and so were not worth robbing.) Their bandy lumbered slowly past the gates of Great Lake, and thankfully the darkness hid them from the sleeping inhabitants of the village. None of them, though, neither the Starry Cluster nor the village inhabitants, had any idea of what else the darkness around Great Lake was hiding.

Preena was a seven-year-old girl who lived in the Hindu temple house in Great Lake village. She had been given to the temple by her mother to be used as a prostitute. Preena's father was dead, and her mother had given Preena to the temple to try to win some favor from the Hindu gods. Once, when Preena was five, soon after she'd arrived at the temple, she had escaped and had run all the way back to her mother's house, twenty miles away. She was sure her mother would be glad to see her again. But she was wrong. To take Preena back now would be to steal from the Hindu gods, and so when some temple women arrived in search of Preena, the mother willingly turned over her terrified daughter to them. When they got back to the temple, Preena's hands were burned with red hot irons as a reminder that she should never again try to run away.

Two years had passed since that time, and Preena had now found out something that terrified her. She was about to be "married" to the gods in a ceremony. She didn't know exactly what that meant, but the idea filled her with dread. But there was no way to escape; she was watched all day long and locked up at night. In desperation she threw herself down in front an idol and begged to die. She didn't die, but the next day one of the older women in the temple house told her about the child-stealing Amma. To show her how safe she was inside the temple and how grateful she should be to live there, the woman told Preena scary stories about Amma and her band of followers. But the stories had the opposite effect on Preena! She began to think there was an Amma out there who would take her away and hide her. How wonderful that would be if she could just find this child-stealing Amma! Preena would gladly take her chances with her and her band of followers rather than stay and be married to a god.

And so, the very night the Starry Cluster was passing by Great Lake village, Preena became strangely alert in the middle of the night. She sat up on her sleeping mat with a sense that something was about to happen. Quietly she crept to the door. She pushed it lightly. Amazingly, it swung open. It was never left unlocked at night. A moment of doubt passed through Preena's mind. Was this a trick to see whether she still wanted to run away? She looked back at the other sleeping girls in the room and gathered her courage. Placing each foot deliberately, she stepped out of the room and into the courtyard. Once again she found a door unexplainably open. She looked around for any sign of the night watchman. He was not around, so she crept out of the temple grounds and into the street. She started to run, faster and faster, out of the village and toward the bridge that led to Pannaivilai. She followed the exact same route Jewel of Victory had taken when she had fled to be with Amy four years earlier. And like Jewel of Victory before her, once she reached Pannaivilai, Preena didn't know where to go. Out of breath from all her running, she walked around until she came to the local Christian church.

She stood in the darkness outside the church and patiently waited for something to happen. After a while something did happen. Even though it was very late, a Christian woman whose name in English was Servant of Jesus came out of the church. She saw Preena and knew immediately she belonged in the temple. But Servant of Jesus didn't want to cross the bridge in the dark and take Preena back to where she belonged, so she took her home for the night. She planned to return her to the temple first thing in the morning. But Preena would not sleep. She kept telling Servant of Jesus she would not go back to the temple and that she needed to find the child-stealing Amma.

Servant of Jesus didn't know what to do. She knew that Amy and the Starry Cluster were not at home; they had been away for a year. Obviously, it was going to take quite a bit of effort to get the stubborn little girl back to the temple. Even though Servant of Jesus was a Christian, the thought of keeping Preena and not sending her back to the Hindu temple never even entered her mind. Sheltering a child who belonged in the temple would almost surely get her killed.

By morning, Servant of Jesus had been worn down by Preena's nagging to see the child-stealing Amma. Even though she had told the girl over and over that Amma was away on a trip, Preena would not believe it. So at 6:30 in the morning, to prove her point, Servant of Jesus took Preena to the house where the Starry Cluster lived to show her that no one was there. To her utter amazement, a bandy was standing in front of the house, and Amy herself was sitting on the veranda drinking tea. Preena let go of Servant of Jesus' hand and ran up the steps. She climbed straight into Amy's lap and threw her arms around her neck. It was as if they were long lost friends. Amy didn't know what was going on, but she knew in her lap was a little girl who needed her love. So she threw her arms around Preena and held her close. Servant of Jesus told Amy all she knew about Preena, which was not very much.

Of course, the temple women soon came to claim her, but if there was one thing Preena knew, it was that she would not go back to the temple. She stood in front of the hundred or so people who had gathered to witness the confrontation between

Amy and the temple women and boldly told them she would not return to the temple; she belonged with the Starry Cluster now. After many days of harassment, the temple women finally retreated. They promised to return with Preena's mother and get her back, but for some reason her mother would not come. No one else from the temple came back, either. And so the matter was settled, and Amy had a seven-year-old girl to teach and love.

Another event at this time brought even more happiness to Amy and the women of the Starry Cluster. It was Arulai's baptism. It had been more than two years since Arulai had set down her water jar to listen to the Starry Cluster sing and preach on the streets of her village. Now, finally, her father had given his permission for her to be baptized. A very tolerant Hindu man might allow a female in his family to read a Bible; he might even allow her to pray a little; but to be baptized was different. To a Hindu, baptism marked the point of no return. It was the total, final way to break caste. And yet Arulai's father had given his approval for his daughter's baptism. Amy was truly amazed.

After a year away from Pannaivilai, it was a glorious return. The very morning Amy arrived back, God had led a small child out of the temple right into Amy's lap. And now Arulai had been baptized with the full permission of her father. These were things Amy had been praying about for a long time. But soon afterwards, they came dangerously close to being undone.

Arul Dasan, Arulai's cousin, had joined the men's equivalent of the Starry Cluster which Iyer Walker had formed. After Arulai's baptism, Iyer Walker felt strongly that Arulai and her cousin should have the opportunity to visit with their families, and so he set about making the arrangements. Fortunately, he knew one of the chief elders of the village, a man with considerable authority. The man was old now, but in earlier years he had turned to an Englishman for help with a situation. As a result, he was open to helping other English people in return for the kindness and favor that had been shown him. Iyer Walker met with the old man, who gave his word the children would be safe if they came to visit their families again.

Unfortunately, the old man had underestimated the anger of the people in the village toward Christians. No sooner had the bandy carrying Arulai, her cousin, and Iyer Walker entered the village than a riot broke out. The bandy was tipped on its side and the driver dragged out and beaten with sticks. Iyer Walker was abused and pelted with rocks. In the midst of all the confusion, the two children disappeared. As rocks bounced off him, Iyer Walker prayed hard. Without some help, it seemed unlikely that he or the driver would make it out of the village alive, and certainly not with the children.

Suddenly, everything fell silent. The rocks stopped crashing against Iyer Walker, and the sticks stopped pounding on the driver. All eyes turned in the direction of a man standing under a nearby veranda. Iyer Walker recognized the man as the son of the village elder. With all the authority of his father, he barked out orders, and amazingly, the crowd obeyed. Most were told to leave the area, which they quickly did. Then another man appeared, holding Arulai and Arul Dasan roughly by the back of their clothes. He let the children go, and they came running back to Iyer Walker. The young man ordered the bandy to be tipped back upright. Iyer Walker hurriedly loaded the children into the back of the uprighted bandy and guarded them from behind. The driver dragged himself from the ground where he lay bleeding and crawled into the front of the bandy. The young man waved them on. The driver flicked his whip, and the oxen turned slowly and headed out the village gate.

When they got back to Pannaivilai, Amy was shocked by what had happened. She had thought they had a good relationship with Arulai's father in particular and that he would be glad to see his daughter. Amy was still learning just how much every aspect of Hindu life was ruled by caste. As it turned out, when Arulai's father gave his permission for her to be baptized it meant he was washing his hands of her completely. Attempting to get Arulai and him to talk to each other was impossible. It would be breaking caste for him to even acknowledge he had a Christian daughter.

Fortunately, no permanent harm was done by the "visit," and both of the children were safe. Neither Amy nor Iyer Walker knew it at the time, but both Arulai and her cousin, Arul Dasan, would play vital roles in the amazing events that were just beginning to unfold around them. All Amy knew at that moment was that she had a feeling something big was going to happen. She just didn't know what it was.

Chapter 14

Tied Feet

The Tamil language has an old saying: "Children tie the mother's feet." It means that when a woman becomes a mother she is no longer free to do all the things she had done before. It is as though her feet are tied together and she cannot go far from home.

Amy did not want to be a mother with tied feet, but by June 1902, she was Amma (mother) to Jewel of Victory, another teenage girl named Jewel of Life, Arulai, Preena, and four other baby girls who had been given to her for one reason or another, mostly because they were girls and not valued in Indian society. Amazingly, all of this responsibility hadn't slowed Amy down. Her feet were definitely not tied. She took the eight girls with her wherever she went. They all bobbed along together in the bandy, rolled out their sleeping mats side by side in the tent, and sang songs and read in quiet moments between preaching events. It seemed that Amy had enough energy to do it all.

That is, until July, when Arulai became seriously ill again on one of their journeys. The illness started with headaches and fever, and Arulai was soon diagnosed as having typhoid fever, a sure killer of children in that part of India. Amy and Arulai, along with the other girls and the women of the Starry Cluster, rushed back to Pannaivilai. When they arrived, an around-the-clock team was set up to nurse Arulai. For the next three months everything centered around caring for her in the hope she would be one of the few children who recovered from typhoid. Amy was never far from her bedside, praying for her or singing to her. Despite all the care, however, Arulai caught pneumonia as well. When her temperature plummeted to ninety-five degrees Fahrenheit, Amy called the doctor. After he had examined Arulai thoroughly, the doctor pulled Amy aside. His eyes were sad. Gently placing his hand on Amy's arm, he spoke. "You're going to have to prepare yourself to give her up."

Amy was heartbroken. She loved Arulai as she would have loved her own daughter. More than anything else, she wanted her to get better. Yet the doctor had seen hundreds of cases of children with typhoid fever and knew that when they got this sick, death was certain. Amy sat with Arulai, holding her hand tightly hour after hour. She prayed and prayed that God would perform a miracle. Days passed, and Amy began to wonder whether Arulai wasn't a little stronger than she had been the day before. Then Arulai opened her eyes and asked for water. Soon she was able to lift her head off the pillow. Bit by bit, she was getting better! Amy's prayers had been answered. It was like having her daughter back from the dead.

As Arulai continued to recover, Amy began to think. With the eight children all in one place, a lot of things were much simpler and more organized. With less time spent traveling, the older girls had settled into a routine of helping the younger ones with their reading and math. The meals were also a lot easier to prepare in a cooking hut than over an open fire at the side of the road. And, of course, the children were a lot safer. Living together in the house, they had much less chance of being robbed or beaten than when they were camped at the side of the road out in the countryside.

As much as she liked to travel and share the gospel message, Amy could see that it made more sense for her to settle down and raise the eight girls. On the other hand, Amy was not one for doing the "easy" thing. There were hundreds of thousands of people in the district who needed to hear about Jesus Christ. There were also other temple children like Preena who needed to be rescued, and there were new converts who needed to be taught more about the Christian faith. It was very difficult for

Amy to think of exchanging all of that for being an Amma. Mothering was not traditional missionary work. But was it wrong to think of being a mother to these girls God had so obviously sent to her? Could that be the real missionary work He had for her in India?

Amy wrestled with the question as she nursed Arulai back to full health. Could she be a good Amma to the children and still keep up the same breakneck pace she always had? Or did God want the children to "tie her feet"? The more she prayed about it, the more she knew the right answer. It was time to settle down and give the girls a home. Amy discussed the issue with the women of the Starry Cluster. They, too, agreed that it was time for Amy to stay home and be Amma to the girls. They also pointed out that it was time to find a larger home to live in. With fifteen people piled into the house in Pannaivilai, there wasn't much spare room to move around in. But where would they go to find someplace larger? There certainly wasn't anywhere large enough around Pannaivilai. Besides, who would want a group of caste-breaking Christian women harboring "runaway" girls for a neighbor? No Hindu in his right mind would want this group living next door.

No sooner had the women started thinking about where they might go to find more living space than the answer came. When Iyer Walker had taught the Bible students at Dohnavur, he had been filling in for a missionary who was visiting Australia. But the missionary had never returned to India, and the Bible students desperately needed a permanent teacher. The Bible school was run by the Church Missionary Society, and the group begged their old chairman, Iyer Walker, to come back to Dohnavur and take over the Bible school. If he did, he could have the run of the entire school compound and do with it as he saw fit. Iyer Walker decided to accept their invitation the same week that Amy and the Starry Cluster started praying for God to lead them to a new home.

Of course, Iyer Walker invited Amy and the Starry Cluster to move with him and his wife to the Bible school at Dohnavur, and the women gladly agreed to go along. It was a perfect solution in so many ways. The mud huts at the school were in great need of work, and the land itself was dusty and uncared for. It had been a long time since anyone had done any gardening on the property. But Dohnavur was a safe place to raise children. The village had been founded over fifty years before. In 1827, Charles Rhenius, an early missionary from Prussia, had been very successful in his work in the south of India. He was one of the first men to think about educating Indian women, and he spoke out against the caste system, which he saw as a way to keep poor people from ever improving themselves. Because of his views, Rhenius had encouraged new converts to break caste, and many of them did. Of course, this led to many problems. Christians were drugged, beaten,

or starved to death by their families. The lucky
ones were thrown out of their villages and told
never to return. But where would they go? Charles
Rhenius wrote to his supporters in Europe asking
for help. Money was sent, and tracts of unused
land were bought and called "villages of refuge."
Count Dohn, a nobleman in Europe, sent money to
set up one of these villages, and Charles Rhenius
had named the new village Dohnavur after him.

Most of the people who now lived in the village
had all but forgotten their Christian heritage. But
the village was still a safe, wonderful place to raise
children. It was well off the main traffic routes that
passed through the district. Despite Dohnavur's
being out of the way, within about a five-mile radius
were about fifty other villages. Amy and the Starry
Cluster had a huge mission field to tend within just
a couple of hours' bandy ride from Dohnavur.

As soon as Arulai was well enough, the women
and girls made the move. The Starry Cluster's few
possessions were loaded onto a bullock cart for the
trip west to Dohnavur. The women all knew the
place well. After all, the whole Starry Cluster had
spent the previous year there with Iyer Walker,
although Amy hadn't had as many children then.

Finally, the Bible school came into view. A low
mud brick wall circled the entire compound. A bungalow was on the property, as well as a row of small
rooms, each with a single window. There was also a
whitewashed church where Iyer Walker would hold
his teaching sessions. As the group approached the

school, Amy was grateful that earlier inhabitants of the property had planted a row of tamarind trees. The trees had now grown into a line of majestic shade trees. Apart from the tamarind trees, nothing else useful was growing. The soil was as dry as sawdust. It would take a lot of work to get the school compound to match the plans Amy had for it!

Amy and the Starry Cluster moved into the bungalow, which was to be their new home. They had scarcely unpacked when Amy had to leave for six weeks. She had promised to join Iyer Walker in leading a series of Christian meetings in Trivandrum on the southwest coast of India. Amy loved being by the sea again. It reminded her of the many days she had roamed the seashore as a child back in Ireland.

Iyer Walker and Amy were the two guest speakers, though many times they were more like guest "yellers." With more than two thousand people present, they had no other way to amplify their voices than to yell as loud as they could while they spoke. It was an interesting experience for Amy. It was the first time she had been out of the Tamil region of India in seven years, and she often had to use an interpreter to speak to people attending the meetings. She hadn't realized how used to speaking the Tamil language she'd become. She also hadn't realized how a mother felt being away from her children for six weeks. She had left Ponnammal in charge of the children and the Starry Cluster, so she wasn't worried about their well-being, but she missed them all very much.

Amy couldn't wait to get back to her new home, and when she arrived, many little arms were outstretched to welcome her. Finally, she knew this was the work God had given her to do in India. He had tied her feet, and she was glad. Although many other groups asked her to be their guest speaker, Amy never left Dohnavur without the children again.

There was so much to do at Dohnavur, and the first year sped quickly by. The Starry Cluster continued to preach in the nearby countryside, but Amy's days were taken up with teaching the older children and tending to the babies. Iyer Walker helped out whenever he could, and he was always there to give Amy advice when she asked for it. Amy felt as though she had her own big brother to lean on. But Iyer Walker had his own personal problems to deal with. His wife was very sick, and he had been advised to take her back to England for a year of rest. Reluctantly, in November 1903, he left Dohnavur for England.

For the first time since becoming a missionary, Amy, a single woman, had to carry the entire weight of the ministry alone.

Chapter 15

Little Gems

Amy continued caring for the children and over-seeing the Starry Cluster, but she felt frustrated. It was as if the work she felt called to do was just out of her grasp. Preena had told her many stories of the temple girls. Some of the girls came as new-born babies to be trained for life as temple servers and prostitutes. Usually they were given to the temple by their parents to gain favor with the Hindu gods. Sometimes, if a girl was poor and no husband could be found for her, she was given to the temple to get rid of her. In India, most girls were pledged to marry by the time they were six or seven years old, and most were married by age twelve.

The whole situation sickened Amy when she thought about it, but what could she do? How could she get access to these girls? They were prisoners, shut in behind locked gates and watched every minute of the day. All Amy could do was to let other Christians know of her willingness to help and to pray and wait for God to crack open the door for these girls as He had for Preena. Amy sent letters all over India to let pastors and missionaries know that if they rescued any temple girls, Amy had a place of refuge for them.

Then on March 1, 1904, Amy's frustration began to lift. Her prayers were finally answered. A small, wizened bundle was thrust into her arms by a pastor from the north. He had heard of a newborn baby who had been given to the temple, and he had mounted a daring rescue. Then he had traveled through the night to bring her to safety at Dohnavur. Preena, who had been with the Starry Cluster for three years now, had the privilege of naming the new baby. She chose the name Amethyst, after the precious purple gemstone.

It was a hard fight to save Amethyst's life. The baby was very weak, and it was difficult to find milk that was suitable for a newborn baby. But Amethyst was a fighter, and she began to gain strength and started to grow. She was soon followed by another temple baby, who was named Sapphire, after another gemstone. Sapphire had also been saved by an Indian pastor. She was a round, happy baby and didn't require as much nursing as her "sister" Amethyst.

Amy's family was growing rapidly, and she couldn't have been more pleased. By June 1904, six months after the Walkers left for England, Amy had seventeen girls to look after. Six of the children had been rescued from Hindu temples. Of course, there was not nearly enough room for "the family" in the bungalow, but they all made do with what they had. A long, low mud brick hut next to the bungalow served as the nursery, kitchen, and dining room rolled into one.

Not only was space in short supply, but having so many children around meant an incredible amount of work. Piles and piles of laundry had to be washed by hand and hung out to dry. Buckets of rice had to be cooked, and mounds of vegetables needing to be chopped up. Then there were the thirty bedrolls that needed to be aired and rolled up each morning, not to mention schoolwork to be collected, floors to be swept, and maintenance of the buildings to be done. The list of chores went on and on.

The Starry Cluster worked alongside Amy, though at times it was difficult for them. Since birth, most of them had been raised with the idea that certain tasks were for certain castes. Even as Christians they found this idea not easy to overcome. It was very humbling for the women of the Starry Cluster to wash clothes for others, sweep floors, and burn trash. Most of them had been raised "above" such things. Amy had to keep reminding them, and herself, that Jesus had washed the dusty, dirty feet of His disciples.

Slowly, the Starry Cluster came to understand that real love means serving others, even little

babies who scream through the night and fuss during the day.

One problem they faced was that some of the
babies were too weak to feed on goat's or cow's
milk and needed to be breast-fed. But finding someone willing to breast-feed another woman's baby
was a challenge. Once Amy found a woman in the
village who was willing to breast-feed a newborn
baby to save its life. The woman knew she was
breaking caste in doing so, but she did it anyway.
Sadly, it cost the woman her life. Her husband was
so outraged when he found out what she had done
that he poisoned her. After that, it became impossible to find any women willing to breast-feed someone else's baby.

With so much going on, sometimes Amy felt the
need for a break. She would pack a few clothes and
take the older girls with her to Ooty, where she
would go for long walks in the forest with the girls.
It was on one of these walks that she began to think
again about the need for a nursery. She'd thought
about it before, but there was never any spare
money for building. Even though Amy sent a regu-
lar newsletter called "Scraps" to her supporters in
the British Isles, she never asked for money or even
hinted that the family might have special needs. She
remembered back to the time in Belfast when she
had wanted to build the Tin Tabernacle and God
had supplied the money and the land for it. Amy
had decided then that she would never beg for
money. Instead she would wait for God to move

people's hearts to give. In all her years since then, she had never budged from that position, and no matter how difficult things got, she promised herself she never would. The work at Dohnavur would never be expanded on borrowed money or on money unwillingly extracted from people. Even though she'd thought of building a nursery before, she had never felt it was the right time to do so. But strolling in the hills above Ooty, she felt that God was saying to her the time was now right to build.

When Amy got back to her friend Mrs. Hopwood's home, where she stayed on her visits to Ooty, she wrote a note to the family at Dohnavur and asked them to begin making mud bricks right away. It was time to build! Within an hour, the mail arrived at Mrs. Hopwood's, and with it was a letter for Amy that contained a money order for an amount large enough to cover the cost of the bricks. Amy was very excited and could hardly wait to get back to Dohnavur to tell the family the news and start drawing up plans for the new nursery.

When Amy arrived home, another money order was waiting. It was an anonymous gift from someone in Madras with "for the nursery" written on it, but Amy hadn't even had time to tell anyone about the nursery project. The money was enough to buy a field next to the compound to build the nursery on and to pay for the rest of the building materials.

The nursery was well under way when Iyer Walker arrived back at Dohnavur after a year in England. His wife was still not well enough to accompany him back to India, but he did bring someone else with him: Amy's mother.

Mrs. Carmichael had been planning for some time to come to India and see for herself the work her daughter was involved in, and Iyer Walker's return provided the perfect opportunity for her to make the trip. It had been almost ten years since Amy had said a tearful good-bye to her mother in Manchester, England, and mother and daughter had a wonderful reunion. Amy was glad to see her mother after so long. Her mother brought news of her brothers and sisters, now spread out around the globe. She also had news of Robert Wilson, and it was not good. He was frail, and his health was failing quickly. Amy's joy at seeing her mother was tinged with sadness for Robert Wilson.

Mrs. Carmichael fit right in to the extended family. The children called her "Atah," Tamil for grandma, and they trailed her around wherever she went. When she arrived at lunch each day, little posies of flowers were at her place, and when she sat to read in the heat of the afternoon, little hands busily fanned her. Amy was glad to have her mother's advice. Sometimes she was not sure how to care for the littlest babies, especially when they were sick. Because Dohnavur had no doctor, Amy had to do the best she could with very limited medical knowledge.

Mrs. Carmichael had already raised seven babies herself and had invaluable advice for her daughter. It was not long before Amy needed all the advice her mother could give. However, their best efforts weren't enough. Two of the babies stopped drinking. Amethyst, the first temple baby to be brought to them, and one other baby, who had come soon after, got sicker and sicker. Nothing Amy and her mother tried would get the babies drinking again. Within a few days of each other, both babies died.

It was a sad day as a new area of land was set aside: the family's cemetery, which Amy called God's garden. It was a quiet area between the bungalow and the vegetable garden. The two babies were buried there. There were no headstones or plot markers, just the beauty of the garden and the shade of the majestic tamarind trees as silent witnesses to the children's passing.

Sapphire, the round, happy baby had turned into an equally round and happy toddler. She was the older children's favorite. They took turns playing with her and walking her around the compound. However, Sapphire was not well, either, and Mrs. Carmichael watched over her day and night. But again, all her motherly help was not enough, and on January 6, 1905, a few days after the other babies died, Sapphire died also.

Everyone was heartbroken. Three babies were gone. Amy didn't know how to console her family. She took the older girls out into God's garden. As she searched for words of comfort, her eyes rested on a beautiful lily, the first one ever to bloom in the garden. She walked the girls around the garden showing them the convolvulus and nasturtiums that were blooming, and then she stopped at the lily. "If Jesus came into this garden," she asked, "which flower would you give Him?"

The girls pointed to the single lily. "We would give Him this one," they all chimed.

Amy nodded. "God has asked us to give Him three of our most beautiful lilies, and I would not hold them back," she said simply.

While life at Dohnavur went on, it was only a short time later that Amy herself needed to be comforted. News reached her that the Dear Old Man, Robert Wilson, had died on June 19, 1905. Fortunately, Mrs. Carmichael was still visiting and was able to give her daughter the comfort she needed. After grieving for Robert Wilson, Amy threw herself back into the work at Dohnavur. Three new babies soon joined the family, and the nursery was once again alive with the happy sounds of baby girls.

Finally, after nearly a year and half visiting and working alongside her daughter, Mrs. Carmichael returned to England in March 1906. Everyone was sad to see Atah leave. But they didn't have much time to miss her, because the nursery was filled with babies who cried out for attention. Soon everyone was back focused on the growing work that God had given them to do.

Chapter 16

A Strange Sense of Joy

It was three o'clock in the morning on May 10, 1909. Amy sat quietly under a banyan tree. She was partly hidden in the shadows. That was the way she wanted it. She could see about a mile down the moonlit road, but no one could see her. She was waiting for someone, someone she hoped could help her.

It had all started two months earlier when a young girl and her mother came rushing up the steps of the bungalow yelling for refuge. Amy sat them down and poured cups of steaming tea while the mother told her story. Her twelve-year-old daughter Muttammal was her only child. Muttammal's father had recently died and left all his possessions, including several thousand rupees worth of land, to her. That is where the trouble had started.

Muttammal was now a very rich girl, and for her father's family, the most important task was to keep her land and wealth in the family. This, they decided, would be easy. All they had to do was marry Muttammal off to one of her father's relatives. An old man, a distant cousin of Muttammal's father who had no wife at the time, was chosen to be her husband and so secure the family's wealth. Muttammal's mother told Amy she was horrified at the thought of her daughter being married off to someone old enough to be her grandfather, and she had escaped to Dohnavur with her daughter.

Amy immediately offered to look after Muttammal, and her mother disappeared as quickly as she'd arrived. When her mother was gone, Muttammal finally found her voice. "Promise me whatever happens, you will not make me leave here," she begged Amy.

Amy tried to be as reassuring as possible, though she knew there had been times when the Dohnavur family had been ordered by the court to give up girls, and they had done as directed. "I can't promise you that, but we'll do our best," she told Muttammal.

The answer was not good enough for Muttammal. Four years before she had heard of Dohnavur and the Christian God and how He answered prayer. "But I have heard that your God answers prayer. Won't He answer the prayer of a little girl?" she asked.

"Let's pray together and see what happens," Amy answered.

Meanwhile, Amy had found out more about Muttammal's mother, who was not the kind, caring woman she had pretended to be. In fact, she was as greedy as her husband's family. She did not want Muttammal to marry the old man because she was looking for a way to keep Muttammal's money for herself.

Amy was sickened by the way both the mother and father's family viewed Muttammal as a way to get rich. Amy had grown to love Muttammal and felt she deserved to live with people who cared about her.

Iyer Walker had been away when Muttammal arrived, but as soon as he returned, Amy filled him in on the details. Because Muttammal had been left at Dohnavur by her mother to keep her out of the reach of the father's family, Iyer Walker had a bad feeling about the situation. To protect themselves legally, he urged Amy to speak with the local magistrate and seek his advice. Amy did so the next day, and the magistrate told her she should return Muttammal to her mother immediately.

Amy didn't know what to do, but she did not believe in breaking the law. She decided to wait a day before returning Muttammal to her mother in the hope some legal way to keep her might be found. She prayed for a solution, even a miracle, through the night. But in the morning, things were exactly as they had been the night before, and Muttammal had to be returned to her mother.

That is what had led Amy to be under the banyan tree at three o'clock in the morning. She'd heard that a high court official might be passing through on a journey early in the morning. Sure enough, at about 4:00 A.M., Amy heard the rumbling of a bandy in the distance. She stood and waited for it to come nearer. When it was close enough, she darted out of the shadows and flagged it down. The English official riding inside was astonished to see a single white woman in a sari running out to greet him, especially at four in the morning. However, he stopped and accepted Amy's unusual invitation to have a cup of tea and a sandwich. As the official sat under the tree eating his sandwich and drinking his tea, Amy told him the story of Muttammal and how both sides of her family were fighting over her custody to gain control of her inheritance.

The official listened and nodded sympathetically or raised his eyebrows or shook his head at all the right moments. Amy felt sure that he understood. But then he told her the bad news. He was sorry, but there was nothing he could do. India had its own strange and mysterious ways, and it was not British Empire policy to interfere with matters of religion or local custom, no matter how unacceptable they seemed to the English.

Amy thanked him, and after he'd proceeded on with his journey, she wearily packed up her teapot and china cups into a basket and walked back to the bungalow in Dohnavur. As she walked past paddy fields and sleeping bullocks, she tried to think of a solution. Muttammal had such a simple faith in God. Amy was sure something would happen to save her from her terrible circumstances. And something did happen, though it was not what Amy had in mind. Muttammal was kidnapped by her father's brothers. Of course, this made her mother very angry, and she went straight to court to get her daughter back. Eventually, the judge ordered Amy to look after Muttammal at Dohnavur until it was decided which side of her family should get her. There were two conditions to this temporary custody. First, Amy had to promise that Muttammal would not change her religion, which to a Hindu meant she would not be baptized, and second, Muttammal had to keep caste.

The second condition was more difficult to keep than the first. Muttammal was from a high caste and could not eat food cooked by someone of a lower caste or even eat in the presence of a lower-caste person. This meant that she had to prepare and eat all her own food alone in a tiny room. It was an inconvenience for everyone, but Amy tried hard to help Muttammal stick to the agreement with the court.

Muttammal begged Amy to be allowed to stay at Dohnavur for good. Finally, Amy agreed. Someone had to speak up for the child. Amy didn't know how, but she would find some way to gain permanent custody of Muttammal. She would need a good lawyer, though, and good lawyers were very expensive. But Amy managed to find one she could afford. A Christian lawyer from Madras offered to take on Muttammal's case for free! Amy and her lawyer quickly filed for custody, and while court hearings were being continually delayed, Amy and the family grew to love Muttammal even more. Muttammal fit in easily, and although she knew she couldn't be baptized, she became a Christian in her heart.

Time dragged on. Amy kept Muttammal with her nearly all the time. She realized that if the Dohnavur family let down their guard for a moment, Muttammal could easily be kidnapped again. All her father's family needed to do was tie a marriage jewel onto her, and it would be too late; she would be officially married to the old man. As the court case dragged on, it became more and more complicated, more and more costly, and more and more stressful for Amy. She longed for it all to be over.

Muttammal's court case was not the only thing on Amy's mind. The family at Dohnavur was grow-ing rapidly. Amy was now Amma to more than one hundred girls. This meant that more staff were needed, and Amy was thankful when Frances Beath, an Australian missionary, joined the family. There was also a constant stream of visitors to Dohnavur. It seemed people were reading *Things As They Are* and deciding to come to India to see Amy's work for themselves. One person who was visiting at the time was Mabel Beath, Frances's sis-ter. Amy welcomed her as she welcomed everyone who came to visit: She put Mabel straight to work!

Finally, after much delay, March 27, 1911, was set as the day the custody trial would be settled. On the night before, Iyer Walker escorted Amy to Palamcottah, where the verdict was to be read. Amy prayed that God would somehow make a way for Muttammal to stay with them. Muttammal herself had stayed behind in Dohnavur with Ponnammal. Although Muttammal was still safe with the family, Amy knew that if the judge ordered Muttammal to be handed over to her mother or her father's family, she would have to obey his order. As she entered the courtroom, she thought about two nights before when she had stayed up all night talking with Muttammal. Amy had hoped to encourage her, but just the opposite had happened. Muttammal had such a strong faith in God and a trust that things would work out that she had encouraged Amy.

The courtroom was sweltering as the clerk read the judge's verdict. Page after page of elaborately phrased summary was read. Finally, after listening to the clerk read for over an hour, Amy heard the news she had dreaded for nearly two years. Muttammal was to go back to her mother, and Amy had to pay all of her mother's legal expenses for the trial. Muttammal was to be handed over to her mother on April 4.

It should have been a moment of complete defeat for Amy, but somehow it wasn't. Amy felt a strange sense of joy, and somewhere deep inside she knew that everything was going to work out.

Amy's lawyer thought she should appeal the verdict immediately, and so without much enthusiasm for yet another round of court cases, Amy agreed to go to Madras to meet with the lawyer yet again.

The night before Amy was due to catch the train from Palamcottah to Madras, she received a message from Iyer Walker, who had returned to Dohnavur. The message made her trip to Madras unnecessary. It read, "When I returned home on Thursday morning, it was reported to me that Muttammal had disappeared…"

Amy was stunned. Conflicting thoughts rushed through her mind. Had Muttammal been kidnapped by her father's family? Was she already married? Or had she run away? Had someone in the Dohnavur family helped her? And what did this mean for Amy and the rest of the girls? The judge was sure to think Amy had arranged for Muttammal to go into hiding. He could find her in contempt of court and throw her in jail. That could mean the end of the Dohnavur family. Amy hurried back to Dohnavur as fast as she could to find out what had happened to Muttammal.

She questioned everyone, but no one seemed to know anything about Muttammal's disappearance. Ponnammal had seen her go to bed in the evening, but when Muttammal didn't show up for her chores the following morning, Frances Beath had gone to find her. But Muttammal wasn't in her room, and not a single thing of hers had been taken or disturbed. Her bed roll was unwrapped, which suggested she had slept there. Beyond that, Amy could learn nothing more. She was sure no one was lying to her, but she was also sure Muttammal couldn't have disappeared the way she did on her own. It was a mystery.

Amy had plenty of other things besides the mystery to think about. Many people had followed the case of Muttammal, and now that the girl was missing there was a public outcry against Amy and her work. Amy turned to another English lawyer to review the case for her. His advice to Amy was to the point: "I advise you to disappear with all your children and cover your tracks. If you cannot do that, I do not know what else you could do to save them all, except faith."

Amy shuddered. She had spoken up for Muttammal, and now she was in danger of losing her whole family and ending up in a Madras jail. Yet she couldn't forget the feeling of joy that had flooded her when she heard the verdict. Somehow she knew that God would work things out. As it was, she had no other choice but to hold on to her faith. There was no way an English Amma and more than a hundred girls could hide themselves anywhere in India, even if they wanted to!

Amy and the family prayed about the situation every day. They prayed for Muttammal. They asked that she would be kept safe wherever she was, and they prayed that no court case would be filed against Amy because of Muttammal's disappearance. And none was filed. Once Muttammal was gone, her father's family and her mother seemed to lose interest in her, and the whole matter of where she had gone or who had taken her was forgotten. Amy supposed that the families were too busy fighting over the inheritance Muttammal had left behind to care about where she might be.

Amy was still left with a huge legal bill, though. Her own lawyer had donated his time, but Muttammal's mother's lawyer had cost a great deal of money, money Amy didn't have. The last thing Amy needed was to be held in contempt of court for refusing to pay the mother's legal bills in addition to "losing" Muttammal. Just in the nick of time, an anonymous donation arrived at Dohnavur that would cover the legal bills. It was the exact amount needed, right down to the last rupee. Amy was delighted; she knew that God still had His hand on the whole situation.

It was not until October 1911, seven long months after Muttammal had disappeared, that Amy received a letter postmarked from Kwangsi Province in China. Amy tore the envelope open and began to read. The letter was written in Muttammal's neat handwriting and told an almost unbelievable story. The night they had heard the judge's verdict, Muttammal had gone to bed as usual. During the night she had been awakened by Mabel Beath, the visiting sister of Frances. Mabel had taken Muttammal to her room and dressed her as a Muslim boy. Then Mabel had taken her outside the compound and told her to wait. Soon after, a bullock cart lumbered by, and Muttammal was beckoned to climb aboard. Not knowing what else to do, she had obeyed. The driver of the bullock cart turned out to be a Christian from a nearby mission. He had handed Muttammal to another Christian, and so it had gone, passing her from one Christian to another until she had arrived in Colombo, Ceylon. There an Englishman escorted her to Malaya, Singapore, and then to Hong Kong. From there they traveled by junk six hundred miles up the West River to the town of Nanning in Kwangsi Province. In Nanning, Muttammal was delivered to the home of an American missionary couple, Dr. and Mrs. Clift, with whom Muttammal was finally safe and happy.

Amy lay down the letter and smiled. Joy flooded over her with the knowledge that her "daughter" was safe. She wiped the tears of joy from her eyes as she tried to imagine all the Christian strangers who had spent time and money to escort a girl they had never met before on an amazing journey. She thanked God for faithfully watching over one young Indian girl who had put her faith in Him.

Amy tucked the letter into her sari and went to find Iyer Walker, who had been there to support her through all the ups and downs of the custody case. She wanted him to be the first to know the good news about Muttammal.

Amy would not have Iyer Walker to lean on for much longer. In August 1912, he was preaching in a series of meetings at Masulipatam. On August 24, Amy received two telegrams. The first, which had been delayed for two days, said that Thomas (Iyer) Walker was dangerously ill. The second bore the message, "Revelation 22:4." Amy reached for her worn Bible and flipped to the last page. She scanned down to the verse "And his servants shall serve him, and they shall see his face." Amy sat for a long time after reading the verse. It could mean only one thing: Her dear friend who had taught her the Tamil language and supported her through all the trials and tribulations of starting the Starry Cluster and then the family at Dohnavur was dead. He was fifty-two years old when he died, and the news of his death left Amy in a daze. It was so difficult to believe that the healthy man who had left just a week before was dead. As the week went on, Amy heard that Iyer Walker had died of food poisoning. She also had the heartbreaking task of contacting his wife, who was back in England and still very sick.

For a few days, it seemed as though grief might overcome Amy. Iyer Walker had been like a big brother to her, and news of his death had come several weeks after news of the death of her other special friend in India, Mrs. Hopwood, in Ooty. Amy had always gathered a team around her for support and encouragement, but now she was on her own. How would she cope without these special people?

The women who worked with Amy were concerned for her. Ponnammal tried to help. "It is very difficult to see how this is for the best," she told Amy.

Amy replied, "It is not difficult to see how this is for the best; it is impossible. But we are asked to walk not by sight but by faith, and only faith can allow us to let Iyer Walker go without bitterness."

Amy prayed for the strength to go on, and within days of Iyer Walker's death, two new helpers arrived to work alongside her. While they could never fill the gap left by Iyer Walker, they were very helpful. They were two sisters, Edith and Agnes Naish, who had both been missionaries in India for many years. As soon as they had heard of Iyer Walker's death, they had given up their own plans and rushed to help Amy. Both sisters fit into the family perfectly, and Agnes Naish relieved Amy of the huge burden of running the school for the girls.

Arul Dasan, Arulai's cousin who as a boy had been beaten for listening to the gospel message, had been Iyer Walker's assistant for many years. Following Iyer Walker's death, Arul Dasan offered to help Amy in any way he could. With enormous relief, Amy gladly handed over charge of all the building work to him. This involved Arul Dasan's supervising the maintenance of the existing buildings and the planning of new ones. The family was still growing fast, and one hundred forty people were now living with the family, so there was always some kind of building in progress.

Within a year of Iyer Walker's death, Ponnammal became sick, and Amy took her to Nagercoil for treatment. It turned out she had cancer, and two operations were performed to try to get rid of it. Amy stayed with Ponnammal for two months while she recovered. Finally, the doctors said that Ponnammal was well enough to make the journey back to Dohnavur.

Soon after arriving back at Dohnavur, Amy received more bad news. On July 14, 1913, back in England, her mother had died. Again Amy stopped to mourn. But the Dohnavur family was still growing, and Amy threw herself into the work, trying to forget all the tragedy that had surrounded her during the previous year. But it wasn't long before another shadow fell. Ponnammal's cancer returned, and on August 26, 1915, she too died and was buried in God's garden at Dohnavur.

It was a difficult and lonely time for Amy. Ponnammal had been with her from the beginning of the Starry Cluster. She was the one Amy had left in charge of the family when she was away. And just as she had with Iyer Walker, she had come to rely on Ponnammal, but now Ponnammal was no longer there. And just as it had been for her after Iyer Walker's death, Amy had to rely on her faith to go on without bitterness.

As before, Amy threw herself into the work, and the joy of being Amma to so many happy little children rescued from Hindu temples and other desperate situations soon helped Amy to press on after the deaths of so many of the people close to her.

Sometimes Amy had dreams that she learned to pay attention to. In one of her dreams she had seen Muttammal and Arul Dasan being married in a wedding ceremony in Ceylon. The dream was very vivid, filled with little details, like their being married in the Galle Face Church in Colombo and neither Amy nor the Clifts being present. Amy didn't say anything about it for some time, but finally she shared the dream with Arulai. Much to Amy's surprise, Arulai smiled widely. "I have been praying that Arul Dasan and Muttammal would get married for over a year now," she told Amy with great excitement.

Amy asked Arul Dasan what he thought about the idea of marrying Muttammal, and he was very pleased with it. So he and Muttammal began to write to each other, and soon they were engaged. It was thought that Arul Dasan would travel to China for the wedding, but in 1917 the world was at war, and it was unsafe for him to travel all that way. Besides, Dr. and Mrs. Clift were leaving China, and it seemed more sensible for them to take Muttammal as far as Ceylon. The Clifts, though, were in a hurry to get home and were unable to wait in Ceylon for Arul Dasan to arrive for the wedding. So Arul Dasan and Muttammal were married in Galle Face Church in Colombo, Ceylon, without the Clifts or Amy present, just as Amy had dreamed. The newlyweds returned to Dohnavur and set up a home in the compound, where they served together for the rest of their lives. Of course, Amy had a wonderful reunion with Muttammal on her return.

Chapter 17

She Is a He!

A bandy creaked and rumbled its way down the road towards the compound at Dohnavur. Some of the older girls planting rice in one of the outer fields were the first to see it. They rushed to tell Amy that visitors were on their way. By the time the bandy had stopped outside the bungalow, a crowd had gathered to greet it. An old woman climbed wearily from the back of the wagon. She reached in and gently picked up a bundle, which she silently handed to Amy. Amy peeped inside. There lay a little baby, who opened her eyes long enough to see Amy, smile, and then snuggle into her. Amy handed the baby to Mabel Wade, one of her longtime helpers, and invited the old woman in for a cup of tea.

Five minutes later, Mabel Wade came hurrying up the steps and into the bungalow. She was breathless with her discovery. When she had gone to change the baby's wet diaper, she had discovered "she" was actually a "he"! News quickly buzzed around the family that a baby boy had been given to them. They all asked the same question: Could they keep him?

In the India of 1918, this was a very difficult question to answer. Amy had often prayed about a place for boys. While on trips to Madras she had been saddened to see young boys who were trained in the temples to perform plays about the Hindu gods. Their futures were as dark as those of any of the girls before Amy had adopted them. But raising girls and boys together had never been a possibility. For one thing, the boys would have to be kept entirely separate from the girls most of the time. Indian families kept the males and females completely apart. In fact, most Indian houses were divided into a men's and a women's side, and the one group was not allowed to go into the other's rooms. While Amy found that silly, she was careful not to violate too many local customs. That's why, for example, the Dohnavur family never ate pork or beef. Both Hindus and Muslims had such strict rules about not eating certain meat that Amy felt it was a battle not worth fighting. For them to all eat meat would only offend nonbelievers.

Having boys in the same compound as girls was a much more complicated issue, however. How

could Amy put boys and girls in the same class-
rooms and the same dining room without offending
people? Apart from the housing needs, boys
required men to raise them, and there were no men
except for Arul Dasan, who was a good Christian
and a good worker but not a strong leader. Amy
also had been warned that people in surrounding
villages would be more hostile to her if she brought
boys into the family. After all, every family wanted
sons. Sons were much more valued in Hindu society than were daughters. But just as Preena, the first
temple girl in the family, had found Amy, so, too,
had the first boy been thrust unexpectedly on the
family. Amy decided it was God's way of telling
them it was time to start accepting boys into the
Dohnavur family, regardless of what outsiders
thought.

The next day, January 15, 1918, Amy was walking in the field beside the girls' nursery, working
out the dimensions for a boys' nursery. As she
walked, she prayed that God would give her a sign
that it was right to start building such a nursery.
She felt she should ask God for the sum of one hundred pounds to start work on the new building.

At dinner that night, Amy shared her plan with
the other staff members. The next morning they
were all eager to see what might arrive in the mail.
Would a check for one hundred pounds be there? It
wasn't, but one of the workers came to Amy and
said, "It didn't come in the mail today, because it
arrived yesterday! I received a check yesterday from

an inheritance, and it was for that exact amount. God told me to give it to you to begin the boys' nursery." With that, work quickly began on the new nursery.

The newly arrived baby boy was named Arul, after Arul Dasan, and he proved to be a happy and healthy little boy. When he got older, he loved to sit on Amy's knee and have her tell him the story of his "coming" day. "You are my very first son," Amy would start out, and Arul's little chest would pump up with pride.

Despite her many responsibilities, Amy always found time to write. She kept a personal journal, which she wrote in each day, and she wrote books to be printed in England. Most of all she enjoyed writing the stories of people she had worked with and loved. She wrote two books, *The Life of Walker of Tinnevelly* and *Ponnammal, Her Story*. These books, plus her newsletters, which were sent all over the world, combined to make Amy a household name around the world. But Amy never knew it because she seldom ever traveled farther away from Dohnavur than Madras.

Then in 1919, fifty-two-year-old Amy received a telegram from Lord Pentland, the British governor of Madras. It was "good" news. Amy had been awarded the Kaiser-i-Hind Medal for her services to the people of India. Most people would have been excited to be awarded such a medal, but not Amy; she was horrified. She had no idea so many people knew about her work. Her first reaction was to reject the award. She wondered why she should be rewarded for doing God's work. She already had more than enough reward in the love of the hundreds of children she had rescued.

In the end, Amy was persuaded to accept the medal as a recognition of the needs of the children of India. However, nothing and nobody could convince her to attend the ceremony in Madras. Amy hated to have her photograph taken or be the center of attention. Besides, Amy had given her life to raising her children, and something had to be very important before she would leave them for a single night. And to her, receiving a medal from the governor of Madras on behalf of the king of England was not important enough.

Within six months of baby Arul's arrival, a second baby boy arrived, and then a third and a fourth. Arul Dasan and the women struggled to take care of the boys, but it was obvious they needed more men to help with the work. Amy prayed for more male workers, but instead she got more and more baby boys. It wasn't until eight years later, in 1926, when there were eighty boys aged from newborn to fourteen years old, that Godfrey Webb-Peploe arrived to lead the boys' work.

Soon after, Godfrey Webb-Peploe's older brother, Dr. Murray Webb-Peploe, came to visit. He was on his way from India to work with the China Inland Mission. However, China was in the midst of huge political changes, and when Murray Webb-Peploe arrived in Shanghai, he learned that all foreigners had been ordered out of the area he had been sent to. After spending several months in Shanghai, he decided to return to India to help out his brother, and in May 1927, he arrived back at Dohnavur. He offered his services to the family, who gladly accepted them. Amy was sixty years old now, and Murray and Godfrey Webb-Peploe relieved her of much of the day-to-day responsibility for running the Dohnavur family.

Dr. Murray worked out of a tiny grass mat building called *suha vasal*, meaning the "door of health." The mud hut was in fact so small and sparsely equipped that it hardly justified a door on it at all! So Dr. Murray and Amy began to pray about building a proper hospital.

The family urgently needed a hospital for several reasons. First, the ever-growing family had constant medical needs. Second, there was no hospital in the area, and a hospital would provide a wonderful way to serve the villages around Dohnavur. Third, a hospital would give "graduates" of the Dohnavur community a place to learn work skills. This was very important. Amy and the "accals" (elder sisters) and "annachies" (elder brothers) were the only family the children had. Even those children who could still trace their families had been disowned by them. In normal Indian society, girls were usually married off by age fourteen, but Amy did not want arranged marriages for her girls, which meant there were a lot of older unmarried girls at Dohnavur. For Indian boys, being in a family in India meant knowing your place in the caste system and therefore what job you would do when you were older. Since the Dohnavur family had nothing to do with the caste system, there was no way for boys to get useful jobs outside the compound. A hospital would solve the problem. There would be many jobs to learn. Some of the young men and women could become pharmacy assistants, laboratory workers, bookkeepers, and nurses, even doctors.

Amy had a high-quality hospital in mind. It would have an operating room, a maternity ward, isolation wards, and a prayer chamber. The outer wall of the hospital would be lined with tiny cubicles with cooking hearths in them. This was necessary because relatives of a sick person in the hospital would come to cook the food for the person. To keep caste, they had to cook the food in privacy, away from the sight of anyone who might be of a lower caste. Amy didn't agree with the system, but she realized that if she did not provide the cooking cubicles, no one would bring their sick relatives to the hospital.

The hospital plans were expensive. The building was estimated to cost the enormous sum of ten thousand pounds. As usual, Amy would not allow any appeal for money. If God wanted them to build a hospital, she reminded the family, He would provide the money. Plans for the hospital were drawn up, and the family waited and prayed. As they did so, a gift of money came in, but not for a hospital. Instead, it was for a prayer house. An old carpenter in a nearby village had given two months' income to the Dohnavur family to begin work on such a house. He told Amy it was sad that even the tiniest village in Tamil Nadu had a temple or a shrine to the Hindu gods, while Dohnavur had no prayer house for the living God.

Amy began to wonder whether a house of prayer might be more important than a hospital. As she prayed about the matter one day, she felt God tell her that once a house of prayer was completed, He would provide the money for a hospital. Amy made the announcement to the family at dinner that night. A house of prayer would be built first, followed by the hospital. Straightaway, the money flowed in for the prayer house. Some were large amounts, but most were small donations that quickly added up. Even the smallest children in the family were involved in the project. A group of them got together and wrote Amy a note outlining their efforts to save money. Their promise included, "We won't waste soap or leave the soap to dissolve in the water and sun. We won't give out food to the crows and dogs. We won't spill milk."

At last, in November 1927, the family finally had a permanent place in which to hold their prayer and church services. As always, Amy arranged the church services in the new building with the children in mind. The services were kept to half an hour. She knew the children couldn't concentrate for very long, and there was plenty for them to do during a service. The children sat cross-legged in rows, the smallest in the front and the tallest at the back. There was no talking in the building, but the children made plenty of noise when they sang! Amy supplied the smallest children with flags, which they were encouraged to wave in time to the music. The older children were given a drum or maracas to play.

Once the house of prayer was in use, Amy knew the time was right to begin the hospital. Of course, the first thing they had to do was wait for God to provide the money. They didn't have to wait long. On June 28, 1928, the sum of one thousand pounds arrived in the mail. They were one-tenth of the way there! As with the house of prayer, the rest of the money came in smaller amounts. The children themselves even raised some of the money by selling kerosene cans filled with margosa tree berries for half a rupee each. Margosa tree berries could be crushed to get cooking oil from them.

When the hospital was finally finished, it was put into immediate use. People from miles around came for treatment, and many of them were touched to see Christians willingly serve them. Everyone in the Dohnavur family helped with the hospital in some way or another. Some nights even the littlest children would be given brightly colored lanterns to carry. They would walk around the paths carrying the lanterns, sweetly singing Christian songs as they went. Their soft voices would drift inside the hospital and help restless patients to fall asleep.

Amy continued to work tirelessly. She was amazed at how much the ministry had grown from its small beginnings all those years ago in Pannaivilai. She was also amazed after all those years at how much work still needed to be done.

Chapter 18

Amma

Amy stepped from the car and pulled her sari tight around her shoulders. The wind was beginning to whip up, and as she looked at the sky, she realized they would have to hurry. It was about to get dark. Amy and several of the women from Dohnavur were inspecting the renovations to the new dispensary in Kalakada, a village a few miles from Dohnavur.

It was September 1931, and although money was in short supply, Amy felt a renewed interest in reaching out to the neighboring villages. That is what had brought her to Kalakada. Two women from the Dohnavur family had been hoping for five years to set up a dispensary in the village, and now a house had finally been found. At first no one in the village had wanted to rent to Christians, but Amy and the two women had finally worn down a landlord with a "haunted" house that had been vacant for three years. The man had finally rented the house to Amy. Who else was going to rent his haunted house if he didn't rent it to Christians? Once a week, Amy would be driven to Kalakada to see how the renovations to the house were progressing. She wanted everything in the dispensary to be just right for the nurses. On this night, the landlord was not at home, and it was some time before he could be found to let the women into the house.

Eventually, just as the last rays of sunlight were setting, the women were ushered into the house. Amy inspected the new cabinets and shelving. They looked fine. Then she stepped outside to see what progress had been made in cleaning up the yard. She didn't see the hole. All of a sudden she was falling forward. She heard a snap and felt searing pain shoot up her right leg. She lay on the ground in agony. The other women rushed to her aid. They comforted her and kept her still while someone drove back to Dohnavur to fetch a truck. The truck was back in record time, and Amy was rolled onto a stretcher and lifted into the back of it. The truck sped back to the hospital at Dohnavur, where Dr. May, one of the hospital's woman doctors, examined Amy's injuries. She shook her head as she did so. Amy was sixty-three years old and had a badly broken leg and twisted ankle. She needed to be treated by an orthopedic specialist at another hospital. Dr. May gave her a shot of morphine for the pain and sat beside her as the truck bumped its way over the windy road to Neyoor, where there was a hospital with an orthopedic specialist.

The specialist set Amy's leg in a plaster cast and bandaged her twisted ankle. After several days in the hospital, Amy was allowed to return home to Dohnavur. Over the next few weeks, her leg started to heal until she could walk out onto the veranda that stretched across the front of her room. The swelling in her ankle went down so that she could wear her shoes again, but something was still not right. There was pain in her back, and it was not getting any better. In fact, as the rest of her body healed, her back got worse. Dr. May and Dr. Webb-Peploe began to worry. Was something else wrong with Amy? Only time would tell, and it did. The truth, which slowly revealed itself, was that Amy had suffered some irreparable damage to her back during the fall, and as a result she was partially crippled. Even though her broken leg had healed, for the next twenty years she would never again walk more than a few steps or be out of bed for more than an hour or so.

It was a good thing that this truth revealed itself slowly, because it took Amy a long time to get used to the idea of being crippled. Amy had been so active for so long, it was hard for her to accept her new life. At the same time, she loved being in her bedroom, which she called the Room of Peace. The room had an entire bookcase of inspiring books that friends had sent her over the years. Amy hadn't had a chance to read many of them before, but now she did. A huge birdcage was built on the veranda so that Amy could see finches and canaries from her bed. Sometimes Amy even convinced her nurse to let the birds fly free around her room. The birds made a terrible mess, but Amy loved to feed them and have them swoop down and land on her bed. The garden outside her window was kept especially beautiful, with bougainvillea and jasmine twining their way delicately around the pillars of the veranda.

Despite the surroundings and the kindness of people to her, Amy was bothered by the fact she was a burden to people. Since the day she and her brothers had helped the old woman with the bundle of sticks all those years ago in Belfast, she had lived to serve others. Now she needed to be helped almost around the clock. It was very hard for her to accept. Amy was the one who hated to have her photo taken and who wrote stories about herself as if they were another person's adventures so as not to draw attention to herself. Now everyone knew she was sick and needed help. Amy had spent so many years focusing on others, and she did not want the focus on herself. She even found it difficult to talk to her doctors about her health. She would rather talk to them about more important things!

Even from her sick bed, there was something Amy could still do. She could speak up through her

writing. She could still declare to the world the
challenge of India's great spiritual need. For years
her supporters and friends had begged her to write
the entire story of Dohnavur. Now she did so in a
book called *Gold Cord*. And that was only the beginning. As she sat in bed year after year, songs, letters,
poems, and thirteen more full-length books flowed
from her pen.

Her next book told the story of the child who
had always remained special to her, Arulai. The
book was called *Ploughed Under*, and it began with
Arulai arriving on Amy's doorstep thirty-three
years before. Arulai was forty-nine years old when
Amy had her fall. Everyone assumed she would be
the one to take over most of Amy's leadership of the
family. But it did not happen that way. Soon after
Amy's fall, Arulai caught smallpox. She recovered,
but not completely. Sometimes she was so weak she
would lie for days in the bedroom next to Amy's,
and they would exchange notes with prayer items
and Bible verses on them. Over the next three years,
Arulai's health went up and down, until in May
1939, she died and was buried in God's garden
along with so many of Amy's other "children." The
sweet sound of the children as they sang at Arulai's
graveside wafted into Amy's Room of Peace and
filled Amy with both sadness and joy.

Throughout her remaining years, Amy prayed
for her two adopted countries. She prayed for
England. News came in 1939 that Prime Minister
Winston Churchill had declared war on Hitler's

Germany and later on Japan. This was a particularly sensitive matter in the family, because there were some German missionaries working with them.

World War II gathered strength, and by 1942 it looked as though Japan would capture Singapore and possibly move on to invade India. Plans were drawn up for an evacuation from Dohnavur into the mountains should such an attack occur. Thankfully, it never happened. However, just as during World War I, World War II placed a huge financial strain on the Dohnavur community. The price of basic food items like flour and rice increased to nine times their normal price before the war. In addition, mail from England became unreliable, and many checks mailed to Amy never reached their destination. Through all the hardships created by World War II, Amy prayed for her extended family from her Room of Peace.

Amy also prayed for India, the country she loved and had lived in longer than any other. By 1947, India was in the midst of a long struggle for independence led by a man named Mahatma Gandhi, who was just two years younger than Amy. Both of them had a vision for a different India, and both of them stood for many of the same things. Gandhi worked hard to break down the caste system and to educate women. But he worked for change through politics, while Amy worked for change through opening people's hearts to God's love and power.

As India freed itself from England's control, the nation began to tear itself apart. Muslims in the north demanded their own country separate from Hindus, and soon Pakistan was partitioned off from India to become a home for Muslims. Through all of India's turmoil, Amy faithfully prayed for the country.

Through the years, Amy's Room of Peace continued to be a place where people could find wisdom, encouragement, and love. Amy seldom forgot to write a note for a child's "coming day," the day that celebrated each child's arrival at Dohnavur. She was always encouraging the staff members, too. She regularly participated in the leadership of the family from her bed. Even though she had been an invalid for many years, Amy had hundreds of friends who loved her and cared for her. The words God had given her in the cave at Arima, Japan, more that fifty years before were true. He had promised Amy that even though she would not marry, she would never be lonely; and she never was. She was a mother to hundreds of girls and boys, and a friend to many others.

Slowly, Amy's strength began to fade, and her nurse noticed she slept more and more. Then, on the morning of January 18, 1951, she did not wake up at all. A few weeks after her eighty-third birthday, she passed over to the other side, as she so often described death. The leaders and children of the Dohnavur family tiptoed into her room for one last glimpse of their dear Amma.

The family knew what to do next. Amy had made them promise weeks before that they would bury her in God's garden exactly as they had buried those before her. There was to be no extra fuss, no coffin, and no headstone to mark her grave. Just as she had wished, Amy's sari-clad body was laid on a flat board. The children picked hundreds of fragrant flowers and placed them over her until her whole body was under a mound of blooms. At noon her body was carried to the village church. Hundreds of people filed past to pay their last respects to her. And her old friend, Bishop Selwyn of Tinnevelly, hurried to Dohnavur to conduct the public funeral service.

Then, with the bells in the prayer tower chiming out one of Amy's favorite hymns, Amy was gently carried to the Room of Peace for a private farewell among the family. Finally, the board bearing her body was lifted into the air on the shoulders of her "sons." A chorus of little voices sang out the songs Amy had written for them as her body was carried to God's garden. Amy Wilson Carmichael was laid to rest under a tamarind tree in Dohnavur, India. The family had promised not to mark her grave with a headstone, but they hoped she would forgive them for placing a stone birdbath over her grave. It bore a single word: Amma.

Elliot, Elisabeth. *A Chance to Die.* Fleming H. Revell, 1987.

Houghton, Frank L. *Amy Carmichael of Dohnavur.* Christian Literature Crusade, 1992.

White, Kathleen. *Amy Carmichael.* Bethany House Publishers, 1986.

Janet and Geoff Benge are a husband and wife writing team with over fifteen years of writing experience. Janet is a former elementary school teacher. Geoff holds a degree in history. Originally from New Zealand, the Benges spent ten years serving with Youth With A Mission. They have two daughters, Laura and Shannon, and an adopted son, Lito. They make their home in the Orlando, Florida, area.

Also from Janet and Geoff Benge...

More adventure-filled biographies for ages 10 to 100!

Christian Heroes: Then & Now